CW00543493

When is the Millennium?

A biblical critique of "End Times" Theology

Published by

smile
CREATIVE

www.smileprinting.co.uk

Copyright © 2023 Paul Kinney
pauldkinney.com

All rights reserved.

No part of this publication may be reproduced, distributed, or transmitted in any form or by any means, including photocopying, recording, or other electronic or mechanical methods, without the prior written permission of the publisher, except in the case of brief quotations embodied in critical reviews and certain other noncommercial uses permitted by copyright law.

ISBN: 978-1-916266-49-0 (Paperback)

Scripture quotations are from
The Authorized King James Version.

Section One
Introduction
Why I decided to write this   1
Objections to me writing this booklet   2

Section Two:
When is the millennial reign?   5
The proper use of the Visual Aid   6
The Book of Revelation   13
Subjects relating to the millennium   16
The biblical view of the everlasting kingdom   16
The supposed offer of the kingdom   21
The supposed parenthesis   22

Section Three:
World history in miniature   27
The Patriarchs   27
Steven's confession   31
The Parable of the tares   33

Section Four:
Antichrist   37
The Mark of the Beast   49
The binding of Satan   50
Armageddon   53
The Rapture   54
The Great Tribulation   58

Section Five:
The Temple   63
Circumcision   66
The Law   71

Section Six:
What is the premillennial Gospel of the Kingdom   75
The Gospel   77

Section Seven:
The Great white throne   83
Come out of her My people   83

Conclusion   87

Foreword

There was a preacher who was once asked why he had to keep repeating in every sermon, "Ye must be born again". The preacher replied, "because ye must".

If I would wish anything to be emphasised in this booklet, it is exactly that! That is the Good News.

If I will repent of my sins, put my trust in the Lord Jesus Christ, and yield my life to Him, He will save me and I shall be born again "Because ye must".

I'd like to thank all those who helped me get this booklet to this stage. Those who proofread, edited and critiqued, I am not unappreciative.

Paul Kinney, Cushendall, June 2023

When is the Millennium?
A critique of "End Times" Theology

Section One

Why I decided to write this booklet

I decided to write this booklet in response to the many believers I know brought up in Churches teaching the premillennial view of the end times who are now questioning it's validity.

Premillennialism teaches that at some stage in the future an individual will come with a gospel of legal obedience, to reign over this earth and it will be Christ. In fact, the only individual in the Bible who claims to reign physically on this earth, before a new Heaven and Earth, with another gospel is Antichrist, "sitting as God". See the claims of the Papacy also, Catechism 882.

How such a grave error has been allowed to gain a foothold among believers can largely be shown to have come from an erroneous understanding of the Bible's use of types, shadows and symbols etc, which I will also refer to as visual aids in this booklet.

Having grown up in Roman Catholicism I finally came to see that the Bread and the Wine are visual aids, pointing to the One being signified in these elements and that the visible are not an end in themselves. This is the same principle that the Bible applies to all of the visual aids.

Perhaps it is because of my upbringing that I was able to see that it is a similar error being taught in premillennialism too.

Therefore, in writing this booklet, I hope to show how premillennialism makes the wrong use of visual aids, while showing the richness of their proper use, and how the Gospel applies them to us today. We must "hold fast", 2Timothy 1:13, to the one true Gospel, resisting all attempts of Antichrist to undermine it from within the Church, Matthew 10:36, or from without, IJohn 2:16.

For those who do not have access to sound Church teaching, on this or any other subject, I recommend the website metropolitantabernacle.org. "Seek and ye shall find" Matt 7:7.

Objections to my writing this booklet.

Objection has been raised that my writing this booklet will cause further division and confusion. I hope it does not. My intent is that all believers will be united but unity cannot be at the expense of truth. It is precisely because I believe that it is this premillennial error, which is a works-based religion, that will cause the most division and hurt in the end if left uncorrected.

A second objection made was that much has been written on the subject already and by men more capable than I. This is true and I have used much of their material in my research.

However, my purpose here is to provide a more condensed handbook, while still highlighting the failings in premillennial teaching, when compared to God's word. I also found that the books I have read on the subject don't quite nail this point, regarding the principal use of the visual aids. I found those books, while accurate, to be somewhat complicated and more suited to academics. Therefore, I have tried to write in 'layman's terms' using the clearest verses on the subject, so that the topic might be grasped as easily as possible. The fact that the premillennial system itself is confusing shows that it cannot be of God, *ICorinthians 14:9, 33.*

I have included some of my own observations which I hope will be helpful.

A third objection made was that, if this prophetic teaching is for another age, why not just leave it there? Again, it is because I believe that this subject affects souls not only today, but eternally, that it needs to be given serious consideration. Strangely, I find it is the people who say that the millennial reign is for the Jews in a future kingdom who will not leave it there. If premillennialists believe it is for the Jews of the future only, then they should leave them to take care of their own business. But it's not, as it affects us now.

And so, it is out of love for the truth, *2Thessalonians 2:10,* "the body of Christ" *ICor 12:12,* and the glory of God, *Isaiah 42:8,* that I feel compelled to write this booklet.

Writing this booklet has been a great source of blessing to my soul. As I was writing, it started to dawn on me what a privileged time God has entrusted to us. He has appointed us as watchmen, *Ezekiel 33:6,* in these ever, darkening days of deceit and seduction. The darker the world gets, the brighter the light our candle will give off, which will hopefully lead others to light theirs also.

The world is dark because believers are hiding their Gospel light under a bushel, *Luke 11:33.* It has been said, *'It is better to light a candle than to sit and curse the dark'.*

Premillennialism is not the light that will dispel this world's darkness, neither is it the truth that will dispel this world's deceptions. It is our Gospel alone that achieves this, Matthew 5:14.

By speaking to people, I find that many in these dark times are seeking answers and explanations and we must, *"be ready to give a reason for the hope that is in us,"* *IPeter 3:15.*

I understand that I can neither address nor refute every error and variation of premillennialism in detail, in this short booklet. I can only hope that it provides some Biblical principles that the reader can use in their own further studies.

Section Two

When is the millennium? And what is it?

Is the millennium the New Testament Gospel age? Or is it, as premillennialism teaches, a period in the future, when we are to be given "another gospel", in place of, *"the gospel once delivered"? Jude 3.*

Are we wrong today, when we preach that there is only *"one"*, exclusive "way"? Has God's Gospel ever *"returned unto Him void"*, *Is 55:11*, that He should change it?

Was Paul simply advising the Judaizers that their timing was wrong and that the earthly king, and kingdom, they desire, *1Samuel 8:5*, would be along presently?

Did the erroneous offer of a new kingdom and gospel originate with Darby? Or did it originate, in the very beginning, with the Serpent, in the Garden of Eden?

Does God mean us to stop at the visual aids and the letter of the law, or does He mean for us to seek the higher spiritual lesson contained in them, and the spirit of the law?

These are just some of the questions that I wish to address and answer in this booklet.

The proper use of Visual Aids

Heb 9:23-24 "It was therefore necessary that the patterns of things in heaven should be purified with these; but the heavenly things themselves with better sacrifices than these".

The key to answering the questions above lies in understanding God's use of visual aids, which are *"the patterns of things in heaven"*. Premillennialism, however, misses the proper use of the visual aid and instead looks again for their material fulfilment. The Temple and furniture etc, are visible patterns of the Heavenly, they were never meant to be the actual. It is vital that we grasp this.

God has filled His creation with visual aids, all pointing to the spiritual. Because of our weakness, God uses the medium of visual aids and earthly language such as the Parables, as a means to communicate heavenly and eternal truth to mankind. Otherwise, we could never grasp it.

God is Spirit while we are flesh and these visuals are given to aid our understanding of the Word of God which the Holy Spirit then applies to our hearts and minds. He did this with the use of such visual aids as types, shadows, symbols and parables, *"Which are a figure of the true"* Hebrew *9:23-24;* to communicate heavenly truths to us, His nature and how He is to be worshipped.

The visual aid itself had to be purified with earthly sacrifices which were themselves a type, picturing the *"better sacrifice"*, namely Christ, required to purify *"the heavenly things"* V24.

God continually had to remind His people throughout scripture not to make more of visual aids than was intended. These visual aids are now all fulfilled in Christ, "*the true Vine" John 15:1.* Who reveals God's Essence, and is, *"the brightness of His glory and the express image of His Person",* Heb 1:1-3.

One of the disciples said, "Show us the Father", and the Lord responded, "when you have seen me, you have seen the Father" John 14:9 He will go on showing the Divine Nature of the Godhead forever in measures that we can receive, teaching us to worship Spiritually and in truth. God is Spirit. Natural finite minds lack the capacity to encompass His Infinite and Eternal Essence, which the Lord's Human Nature will unfold forever whilst explaining the enormity of Calvary.

The Lord gave mankind glimpses of His Divine Essence at the transfiguration, *Matt 17:1-8,* and in several Christophanies in the Old Testament.

The carnal man misses the Spiritual meaning of the visible, because he is focused on what he sees and finds appealing to his own flesh, wisdom and natural senses.

Premillennialism also teaches that 'literal' means we take the most obvious meaning. I agree, but the most obvious meaning can actually be spiritual, when that is what the context calls for. Premillennialism uses the word literal as though it is the opposite of spiritual, but it is not. Spiritual can be said to be literal also.

It was the job of Prophets, Apostles, teachers and preachers, to explain the spiritual meaning of the visual aid, *Romans 10:14,* thereby teaching man to look for the spiritual lesson being taught in them, *Heb 11:10 "We look for a city not made with hands",* also *2 Cor 5:1.*

God used earthly visual aids in the Old Testament but spoke clearly through His Son in the New *Heb 1:1,* the One who fulfils all that was pictured in the visual aids, *Matt 5:17-22.* Showing that as God and Man, He alone is the true Mediator between the earthly and the heavenly, *1Tim 2:5.*

Being God and Man, He alone could bear the infinite weight of sin and rise again, while every plan where man's weak, fallen, flesh is a link in the chain will snap at that very point. Being Man He was able to take our place. It is only His death on Calvary that can truly explain the history of this world, not a premillennial kingdom of death and sin "for a season" that stops at the visual aids.

Every false religion basically makes the same error as premillennial teaching when they confuse the visible type with the promised heavenly reality.

We have their spiritual meaning clearly explained throughout scripture so that we do not mix them up, *Rom 10:14*. The type is the imprint and shadow left by the true. It is because these God given types were also authenticated by God that much confusion arises for premillennialism.

The first Visual Aids

"When the woman saw that the tree was good for food... pleasant to the eyes, and a tree to be desired to make one wise, she took of the fruit thereof and did eat, and gave also unto her husband with her and he did eat" Genesis 3:6.

In the beginning God created the heaven, declaring His glory, and the earth His footstool. God had made it all *"very good"*, *Genesis 1:31*. However, when Satan fell, he introduced evil into the world and went on to convince Eve that evil is good and good is evil, *Isaiah 5:20*, by shifting their focus from the Spiritual message to the visible.

God had given *"the tree of the knowledge of good and evil"*, beforehand to teach man about evil. In this way he would not have to learn evil through experience, while also learning to do good.

Adam was told not to eat the fruit of the tree to obtain this knowledge, as the tree itself was neither good nor evil. Rather, he was to look for the spiritual message it conveyed.

For when they did eat it, they did not receive any good from it but rather lost it. And the evil they received was for disobeying God by eating of it, Gen 2:17.

Satan persuaded them to override their spiritual insight and to look at the tree with the natural eye and so they lusted after it, which is contrary to God's way *1John 2:16*.

Satan has been using this very tactic ever since which just shows how corrupt man's heart is, that having been taught this for 6000 years we still fall for the same thing.

We see the same trend continuing throughout history with the Heathens and Pagans worshipping the visible Sun etc, not grasping, that *"the heavens, declare the glory of God"*. The heavens teach us about the glory of God but they are not the actual glory of God, just as the tree was not the actual knowledge, but rather it taught about the knowledge of good and evil. Neither is the Temple, nor the Nation, the actual glory of God but teaches us of the glory of God.

Even though the visual aids given to the Jews were more specific in their teaching, for instance Canaan, the Temple, its furniture and sacrifices, giving a clearer revelation of God, man's sinfulness and the Cross work of Christ, the Judaizers still fell for the same old trick of the Serpent when they elevated the National visual aids beyond their true purpose, as premillennialism does today. Their forefathers did likewise, when they worshipped the serpent in the wilderness, 1King 18:4. They were not to worship it but were simply to look at it to benefit, and learn, from it. *Psalm 106:20 "Turning their glory into the similitude of an ox".* The Jewish Nation themselves were a visual aid, picturing all mankind. Most of them were not saved men, with many of them being down right wicked, so they could never be the perfect reality. Rather their purpose, and the Remnant among them, was to teach us that God would always have a people in the midst of this world, the Remnant, the true Israel, who will all be saved Rom 11:26.

When Paul saw converted Jews, who had seen the spiritual reality of the visual aid return like Pagans to them again, he remarked *"I am afraid of you, lest I have bestowed upon you labour in vain"*, *Galatians 4:11,* and he would say the same of premillennialism today, which is also teaching men to return to them, *"Have you need that one teach you again"? Heb 5:12.*

This is also typified in the Roman Catholic system (Catechism Article 3 1322-1327), when they look to the *'Bread and Wine' Mat 26:26-28,* in the hope of receiving eternal life from them, rather than from the One signified in the *"Beggarly elements" Gal 4:9.* Sadly as with premillennialism, they will have their reward in the here and now, if this is where they stop, *Mat 6:5,* with nothing for the future.

2Cor 11:14 Satan continues to bewitch the false religious leaders and teachers of today. He then uses them to deceive their followers into lusting after the visible things of earth, none of which require any true faith or obedience to God, *"Blind leaders of the blind" Matt 15:14.*

1John 2:16 "For all that is in the world, the lust of the flesh, and the lust of the eyes, and the pride of life, is not of the Father, but is of the world". Really these are the only two kingdoms and modes of worship that have ever been in this world *1Cor15:45-47.* One is represented in the seed of the Serpent, who look to the visual aid. The other is in the seed of the woman, who, seeing the spiritual message of "abundant life" John 10:10, being taught, then *"worship in Spirit and in truth" John 4:24.*

God placed enmity between these two seeds, which also helps to distinguish and keep us separate from each other. All in all, there is only one right way and one wrong way, the Broad way, and the Narrow way, so it should not be too difficult to distinguish which is which. One is earthly and man centred, while the other is Christ centred, heavenly and Spiritual.

The Parable of the prodigal son *Luke 15:11,* also sets out these two opposing seeds. One son finds true life, while the other has the land only, *"all that I have is thine"*, he has his reward Mat 6:5.

Paul tried the spirits of the Judaizers *1John 4:1,* and denounced them for turning the hearts of men away from the Gospel, back to the visual aid. The Reformers denounced Roman Catholicism for stopping at the Eucharist instead of trusting in the One signified in the visual aid, "the bread of life" John 6:35. So too the premillennial system must be denounced for doing the same thing, in directing men's hearts back to the visual aids: the Land, the Temple, and the sacrifices, which is simply sophisticated paganism. Luther says to smash the eggs before they hatch into vipers.

Do we lust after the visual aids, or do we see their spiritual meaning, and love God in Christ?

Because men love darkness, *"and receive not the love of the truth God will send them strong delusion"* 2Th 2:11. This is so that their wickedness is highlighted to all.

Without the help of God's Word, man "cannot *distinguish between what is right, and what is nearly right" Charles Spurgeon.* We must search the scriptures *Acts 17:11,* if we are to find the true heavenly meaning of the visual aids, which is their purpose and when we find it, to set our whole heart upon it, *Colossians 3:1.*

Satan knows that he must base his lies on some truth, in order to deceive us, so the offer of the actual, God given, visual aids, is the perfect thing to convince man that they have an end in themselves, thereby causing us maximum confusion. *"Seeing they may see, and not perceive, hearing they may hear and not understand", Mark 4:12.* Of course, what Satan leaves out is the true spiritual message behind them. Premillennialism crumbles when we come to see the proper use and application of the visual aid.

With this in mind, I wish to look at the premillennial method of interpretation in its component parts also, and to show that they each fall foul of and oppose the true Gospel, having no merit at all. The same principles can be applied to every falsehood in religion. God has only ever had one method of salvation, which He has preserved for all posterity. *"Beginning at Moses... expounded... concerning Himself" Lk 24:27.* There is only one race of people Acts 17:26, Jews are not another race.

Premillennialism would have to rewrite scripture, reprogram man's conscience, remove the visual aid, the way of salvation, creation and history, in order to prove their case. *"The truth shall set you free" John 8:32.* Many premillennialists do love the Gospel, but do not realise that they are in conflict.

I realise that what has been said, thus far, may not be enough to convince every adherent of the premillennial system, that it does not adhere to the Gospel plan of salvation. Therefore, I implore you to read the rest of this booklet wherein I endeavour to demonstrate that the premillennial kingdom is an earthly idea, which will fail eternally. Our Gospel message of the Cross is our only hope and foundation, *1Cor 3:11*. Premillennialism is a system *"built on sand"*.

Thankfully, we are not left to ourselves to work all these things out. The Bible, interpreting itself, repeatedly confirms for us that the visual aids were a temporary *"pattern of the heavenly"*.

We have greater light today, and therefore greater responsibility, *Lk 12:48*. It is only if we use the light God has given us that He will entrust us with greater.

Our enemy is craftier than we are but he is not wiser than us if we obey what is clearly taught in the scriptures, *John 7:17*. *"The foolishness of God is wiser than the wisdom of man" 1Cor 1:25,* trust Him.

Is it really so important which millennial view I believe? Yes, it is, for what I believe will determine how I frame my Biblical world view and live out my faith, before those around me. What I believe and do is who I am. If I truly believe that my treasure is in heaven, then I am less likely to feather my nest here.

What we glean from scripture should help us to develop *"a sound mind", 2Tim 1:7,* which will then enable us to discern truth, rather than opening up our minds to the mystic sensationalism that extreme writers are finding in this subject today, which then leads to all this sort of confusion.

The Book of Revelation

Having pointed out the meaning and purpose of the visual aid and before dealing with the subjects relating to the millennium reign of *Revelation 20:6*, I think it is best to look at the Book as a whole where the contested passage is found, a book which premillennialism teaches is written to the Jews.

The first thing to notice is that the name of the Book is Revelation, meaning 'uncover', which shows it cannot be the basis of the confusion taught by premillennialism, *1Cor 14:33.*

Like all scripture, it has been *"written for our learning", Rom 15:4.*

The premillennial confusion arises not only because of their erroneous view of the visual aid, but also because their view is often based on more obscure verses of scripture.

If we were to do a jigsaw, we would start by fitting the obvious pieces together, then the more difficult pieces become easier, and the picture begins to develop. If we do the same thing when reading scripture and start with the clearer verses, then the others fit and start to make sense also. The symbols and visual aids used in Revelation were introduced and clearly explained for us in the Old Testament, and some in the New, so we are not left to speculate as to their meaning. Premillennialism thinks the pieces of two jigsaws are mixed up in the one box.

"Unto the seven churches, write".

The second thing to notice is that the Book of Revelation is written to the Seven Churches *Rev 1:4,* and not to the Jews only as premillennialism teaches. The entire book is written to the Seven Churches, representing the entire New Testament Church, who are warned to watch for Antichrist, which shows that it was not written to so called tribulation Jews either, some 2000 years later.

The early New Testament Church was made up initially of the Remnant Jew, *Rom 11:26.* As a launching rocket jettisons all non-essentials, so the Remnant

Church jettisoned the unsaved Jew along with the Nation's visual aids, which had now served their purpose.

The Theologians identify seven cycles in the book of Revelation, each taking a different look at the New Testament era, proceeding through hills and valleys, yet overall, climaxing in evil, *"The love of many shall wax cold"*, Matt 24:12. First a quarter of the earth, then one third and lastly one half affected, at one time this part of the world, next time another, bringing us up to the end.

Although the characteristics of the seven Churches show us the variety of conditions to expect in the Churches of every age, it is possible that they also indicate the overall climaxing of evil, ending in a Laodicean type of world and church, this would fit with the 'cycles' method of interpreting the Book of Revelation, and the lukewarm inertia we see today. *"Will I find faith on the earth" Lk 18:8.* After more than 2000 years of Church history, I believe it is possible to identify these worsening cycles. Yet in all this, *"The gates of Hell will not prevail against the church" Matt 16:18.* Against the Nation, yes, the premillennial system, and every false religion, also.

The Theologians identify the following sections of the Book of Revelation for us, showing the repeating cycles.

- Chapter 1:1; Opening exhortation *"Shew unto His servants, things which must shortly come to pass. V3 Blessed is he that readeth... the words of this prophesy and keep those things".* How could the reader keep those things, and how could they come shortly, if they are future only?
- Chapters 1-3; regard the character of the Church and how the promises affect the Churches, their strengths, problems and duties, taking us right up to the end and a New Heaven and a New Earth. Each cycle reveals judgement for the world and blessing for the Church, The Lord's victory spelling the demise of the enemy.
- Chapters 4-7; The scrolls: victory over His enemies, as He is found worthy to break open the seals.
- Chapters 8-11; The trumpets: 8:3 offering prayers of the saints, then judgement.

- Chapters 12-14; The woman gives birth: the Dragon is waiting, his Beasts emerge, 14:19 ending in wrath. His Coming to reap (judgement).
- Chapters 15-16; The bowls: Rejoicing with harps in victory over the Beasts 15:2. Babylon receives "the cup of the wine of the fierceness of His wrath" 16:19, while V20 tells us, it is the end.
- Chapters 17-18; The Fall of Babylon and the Beasts. The Second Advent 19:2.
- Chapter 20; Recapitulating on the first five: The Saints reign with Christ, and the Devil to the Lake of fire.
- Chapters 21-22; Elaborates on the final triumph of the Lord and His Bride over their enemies, ending in victory and a New Heaven and a New Earth, which is the consummation of all things.
- Chapter 22:5-7; Closing exhortation *"Show unto His servants, things that must shortly be done". V7 ... blessed is he that keepeth the sayings, of the prophesy of this book"*.

The similarity between the opening and closing exhortations show that the entire Epistle is written to the Seven Churches. So, when we come to Chap 20, if we are to keep it in context, we need to see it as part of one, symbolic, book containing repeating cycles of history to the Seven Churches, and not exclusively for Jews of the future, *John 18:38 "What is truth?"*

If we view Revelation as written in cycles, rather than chronologically as premillennialism does, then the Gospel age can be viewed as the same period that the woman spends in the wilderness *Rev 12:6,* which is the same 42 months (30-day months), trodden down of the Gentiles *Rev 11:2,* and the same 3 1/2 years, 1260 days, that the two witnesses are on the earth V3, each giving a description of the enmity and the differing aspects of the same New Testament period, just as the cycles do.

Incidentally, in *Rev 22:17 "the Spirit and the bride say come",* which places them on earth (not in Heaven as premillennialism would have it) at the same time as the Lord is physically in Heaven. As we all agree that the Lord can never again be separated from His Church *1Th 4:17,* it can only mean that His reign over us now is spiritual, which causes a problem for premillennialism and their chronological system, which they insist is speaking of His physical reign. It causes no problem for us, who say He is with us here and in us spiritually Col 1:27, till the end of the world, *Matt 28:20.*

Premillennialism is also faced with another problem when they take *Chapters 19 and 20*, chronologically. The same scenarios recorded, especially in *19:19-20,* are repeated again in *20:8*, with the deceived and deceivers, facing the final judgement.

Look at the cycles and you will see other examples of this.

Subjects relating to the Millennium.

Having highlighted the problem with the premillennial system as a whole, and having looked at the book of Revelation, I wish to show that the same problem also exists in each individual part, including the contested verse of *Rev 20:4.*

Man has a God given instinct to worship and we will either worship through faith in Christ, *"in Spirit and in truth"*, or lust as the pagans do after the visible, aesthetic things of earth *ISam 16:7*, seeking balm for the conscience from false religious systems of works, that man's wisdom has created.

The Biblical view of the everlasting kingdom.

Rev 20:4 They lived and reigned with Christ a thousand years.

Although we all agree that there is a millennium, the debate regarding when and what it is, can become quite confusing and divisive.

Viewed on the surface, it would appear that the millennium is a period of time that will end 1000 years after it begins.

However, this calls for qualification because, if this were right, we would be able to set a date for when the world will end, (and when it will not), 1000 years after the 1000 years began. Something we know we cannot do, *Mat 24:36 "of that day and hour knoweth no man".*

In order to establish the meaning of a passage we must look at its context in the chapter, the type of book it is in, who it is addressed to, and compare this with scripture as a whole.

Neither do we make a doctrine of a stand-alone passage and as this is found in one passage, in a largely symbolic book, it requires that we seek further light in establishing its meaning.

We agree that the 1000 years is a definitive period of time, but it is a period of indeterminable end. It ends with the Coming of the Lord which is a time we cannot put a date on, hence, the use of the symbolic number 10x10x10, signifying a perfect complete number and period of time. If we also note that 1000 years refers to reign (authority), and not realm, then we will avoid substituting the idea of kingdom, Canaan or realm for the word "*reign*", as premillennialism does.

The Son of God has always reigned, but to have a people to reign over, He had to reverse the Fall and the effect it has on mankind and creation. This He did by His death on the Cross, 2Cor 5:21. To be our "*Kinsman Redeemer*", He had to become Man, as Man He had to be anointed in His Human nature also, *John 17:5*, and so began this unique phase of His continuing reign. On His ascension to Heaven, *Acts 1:9*, He is seated now on His Heavenly throne, at the centre of His realm, where He reigns over all, including in the hearts of those whose faith is solely in Him Ephesians 2:8. He will reign there, at the centre of His realm, until the restoration of all things, *Acts 3:21, and then forever* in "*a New Heaven and a New Earth*", Rev 21:1.

A premillennial kingdom would neither reverse the Fall nor fulfil an everlasting promise, and would also require the death of the "*Testator*" again, to ratify their covenant, *Heb 9:16-17*. A change in covenant would also require evidence similar to the bringing in of the Old and New Testaments, in order to prove its authenticity, *2 Cor 12:2*.

It is only as "*Kinsman Redeemer*" *Ruth 1-4*, for the whole world that He can reverse the Fall. Hence His incarnation, the anointing of His Human Nature *Acts 4:27*, His death and resurrection and reign at the right hand of the

Father. Unfortunately, not all men will avail of Him as Saviour. Many Jews appeared to keep the outward rituals, whose hearts were not right toward God.

Col 1:16 "All things were created by Him, and for Him".

"The everlasting kingdom", therefore, has this unique spiritual phase within it when the Lord begins His reign as God and Man, which covers from the Lord's First Advent to His Second Advent, when He will come again and restore all things to a more glorious position, continuing His reign forever as God and Man over a people and realm then glorified. There is never a time when He does not reign.

There is much scriptural evidence, that His spiritual kingdom has come and therefore that He reigns here now, *Mt 12:28 "If I cast out devils by the Spirit of God... the kingdom of God is come unto you".*

Until His return, He has left us the Holy Spirit as Comforter, *John 14:26,* which again shows that His kingdom in these last days is primarily spiritual. We are justified in Christ, sanctified by the Spirit and glorified by the Father at last. It was *"expedient"* for the Church that the Lord went away, *John 16:7,* it had nothing to do with a parenthesis, or a premillennial kingdom concerning the Jews.

Strangely, premillennialism insists that for the Lord to have any power to reign now, He would have to be visibly present John 11:21, yet all the while insisting that Satan reigns now, because of all the world's problems, though he is not visibly present.

Would the same logic not suggest that the Lord does reign, because of all the good in the world?

Louis Berkoff, 'Christ's kingship is twofold: spiritually over His church, and Kingship over the universe'. While Peter was a pillar of the Church, he was given the keys of the kingdom also, *Mat 16:19.* The Philadelphian Church is also said to have "the keys of David" Rev 3:7, all of which shows believers in the kingdom and in the Church to be a combined entity.

The premillennialists guided tour through their chosen verses is another attempt to draw man's focus away from the one true Way.

1Cor 2:13 "Comparing spiritual things with spiritual".

God first brought His material realm into existence in *Gen 1:1,* and its citizens in *Gen 1:26.* Eve then believed the Serpent, who is introduced to us in *Ch 3,* when he offered her another way, based on her own efforts, a shortcut to godliness, "be as gods". And death did follow, as they had been warned, causing the need for a renewed heart and realm.

Our bodies will die, but thankfully God in mercy has devised a way whereby our souls need not die too. It is the only Way whereby He can remain Just, while showing pardoning mercy to sinners.

This plan will restore all and more, raising man to an even higher relationship in Christ, one which the Serpent unwittingly, and despite himself, played a part in bringing about.

"I will put enmity between [a] thee and the woman, [b] and between thy seed and her seed; [c] It shall bruise thy head, and thou shalt bruise His heel." Gen 3:15.

The enmity between Satan and the woman, the seed of Satan and her "seed", which is Christ, and those in Christ, would involve persecution for us but the outcome would be victorious for Christ and all His people, not a failed premillennial kingdom, which they say the Jews had rejected once before. *Rom 12:2 "Be not conformed to this world".*

God's kingdom is understood by the eye of faith and entered by a Spiritual new birth, while it is Satan's which is of this world, seen with the natural eye, and entered by natural birth, Jewish or otherwise. The Lord alone was manifest to destroy the works of the devil, *1John 3:8.* In the premillennial description of their kingdom, the works of the Devil are not destroyed, *Heb 2:14.* Sin and death do enter their kingdom. While we are not of this world but strive to overcome it, premillennialism promotes its *"broken cisterns"*.

The carnal man does not need any encouragement to strive for these material possessions and positions, *Philippians 3:19 "Who mind earthly things".*

The premillennial kingdom is little more than patriotism, coveting visible 'Real Estate', *"which is idolatry" Col 3:5.* As John Blanchard says, speaking on false religion, 'It does not rescue any from their spiritual enemy, it does not change the nature of the sinner, nor reconcile to God, and deliver from Hell'.
It offers temporal benefits only, whereas we glean a message which is spiritual food and life for our souls, which the Word, creation, our conscience and the Holy Spirit all affirm.

We, as believers, are strangers and pilgrims on this earth, sojourners, whose conversation is in Heaven, Phil 3:20-21, anticipating the paradise of God. It is not so difficult to see who is quite at home here and who is not. There are not two places of Paradise either, Luke 23:43.

I believe God allows the same pressures of life to come upon us all. Unfortunately, the cares of the world will overcome many, *Mk 4:19.* It is only those who ask for His help who can overcome and see through the cares of this world, *"We are more than conquerors" Rom 8:37.* However the insincere who are deceived will not ask for God's help because they *"love darkness"* and the things of this world, and will thereby reap what they sow.

Abraham, believing the Gospel, Gal 3:8, became part of the Remnant Church Acts 7:38.

The Judaizers on the other hand, displaying all the enmity "of their father the devil", John 8:44, were told not to say that Abraham was their (spiritual) father Mat 3:9, even though he was their natural father (only).

Even the Apostles did not understand the true nature and spirit of the kingdom of God at first, *Lk 9:54-55 "Wilt ... we command fire to come down from heaven, and consume them? V55 Ye know not of what spirit ye are",* yet this is the spirit of premillennialism and the same spirit of Antichrist. Or as Ligonier Ministries puts it "Peter would bypass the Cross and choose the crown". The premillennial system would have us do similarly. The Lord's response to Peter was, "*Get thee behind Me Satan*".

The Roman Catholic church, in their 2nd Vatican council document, says that "Christ's death covers all men who follow their own religion faithfully". This can only be what premillennialism is claiming for its system, as it is a different religion from the Christian faith.

There has been no instruction given, to go into all the world and preach the gospel of a premillennial kingdom, *Mk 16:15,* which is but for a season *Heb 11:25.*

Premillennialism thinks far too highly of man and this world, which is to think too lowly of Calvary. The Lord came into the world to save sinners, He did not need to come and die for an earthly premillennial kingdom, whose citizens are not "in Christ". Death was always to be the climax and end to His earthly ministry, not a premillennial kingdom. *"Slain before the foundation". Rev 13:8.*

The supposed offer of the kingdom.

Mat 19:23 "... a rich man... hardly enter into the kingdom of <u>Heaven</u>. V24 "It is easier for a camel to go through the eye of a needle, than for a rich man to enter into the kingdom of <u>God</u>."

Premillennialism would have us believe that there are two people and kingdoms of God, that the Lord came to offer the earthly "kingdom of God" to the Jewish Nation and that "the kingdom of Heaven", is reserved for the Church. *"Is Christ divided"? 1Cor 1:13.*

Yet we can see from Matt 19:23-24 above, that they both refer to the same kingdom. Heb 11:40 also tells us that every believer throughout history will be in one kingdom together.

Eph 3:6 also shows clearly that the saved of the Old Testament and the saved of the New Testament, are all one people of God, whether they were born

Jew or Gentile. Again in 4:4-5 "*There is one body, and one spirit... V5 One Lord, one faith...*" *Lk 13:28* tells us that the Church shall "*see Abraham and Isaac, and Jacob, and all the prophets in the kingdom of <u>God</u>*". We will be there together, there are not two separate eternal existences.

While Matt 8:11, tells us that "*Many shall come from the East and the west, and shall sit down with Abraham, and Isaac, and Jacob, in the kingdom of <u>Heaven</u>*".

Notice that Abraham is in the kingdom of <u>Heaven</u> and in the kingdom of <u>God</u>: we are all "*partakers of the same inheritance*" *Col 1:12.* All this disproves premillennial teaching.

The Lord also told Nicodemus, the Old Testament Jewish teacher, that he "*must be born again*" (indwelt of the Spirit) if he is to see the kingdom of God *John 3:3.* What then had become of the unconditional covenant? Or what about Nicodemus' Jewish nationality? If premillennial teaching is correct, then he would surely have known and argued the point that he was fine. This encounter took place long before premillennialism says the kingdom was postponed.

This same kingdom is also said to have entered within every believer, *John 17:21.* It is the seal of the Holy Spirit and the promised reality that is within each believer. But how can a material premillennial kingdom enter into any one? It is Spiritual life within that we all need, not more earthly life.

In *Mk 1:15* the kingdom is said to be "*at hand*". Again, in what way can it be said that a premillennial kingdom is at hand? In John 17:20 it is said, the kingdom "*comes not with observation*". But how could a 'literal' premillennial kingdom come without observation? When all this is taken together, it clearly shows the kingdom spoken of is a spiritual one and not an earthly, premillennial kingdom.

The supposed parenthesis.

Premillennialism teaches that the Church age is an interruption of the Jewish 'kingdom', a kingdom which was supposed to have been given to their Nation unconditionally. If it was unconditional, then it could not have been postponed, nor taken from them, for any reason. The fact that one Jew is taken in *Matt 24:40*, and another Jew left, also proves that there is not the unconditional covenant for Abraham's natural seed that premillennialism speaks of.

Also, for the kingdom to be postponed the Jews would have to have it already, so, why would the Lord be offering it to them again? This is a paradoxical contradiction which premillennialists cannot explain. The only valid explanation is that the Nation did not have the spiritual kingdom, which the Gospel speaks of. It is the same spiritual sceptre and plan of salvation that proceeds from the Old Testament into the New Testament, while it is the differing modes of administration that change and are therefore taken from the Jewish nation. The way of salvation remained opened to every individual, while the National privileges were taken from them.

What had happened was that the Nation had apostatized and could no longer be used as a visual aid, representatives of the plan of salvation, at the same time as Christ came and fulfilled all.

All that being so, the Jews did not then reject a material kingdom at the Lord's first Advent, because it was never offered to them. Why would they, if that is what they had been waiting for? It was in fact the Lord and the plan of salvation and a spiritual kingdom that they rejected, *"We will not have this man to reign over us" Lk 19:14*. Never once did they say they did not want an earthly kingdom.

They rejected any notion that they were equal to Gentile 'dogs', in need of spiritual deliverance, 1Tim 1:15. They wanted a Messiah who would deliver them from the Romans and restore the status they believed they previously had in this world. They had no thoughts of a Spiritual kingdom. What use would Canaan be to lost souls anyhow? *Mark 8:36.*

It was not Canaan that was taken from them in 70AD and given to a nation bringing forth (spiritual) fruit, *Matt 21:43*. They remained in Canaan when the sceptre, representing the spiritual kingdom, was taken from them and given to the Church. The Church were not given the land of Canaan. *"My kingdom is not of this world" John 18:36*, it is not a material kingdom that was passed on to us.

Lk 9:27 "There are some standing here, which shall not taste death, till they see the kingdom of God come". Those that were born again of the Spirit of God did see the Kingdom of God come, *John 3:3.*

Just as an unconditional covenant cannot be postponed, neither can an everlasting kingdom be a parenthesis. The preaching of the kingdom of God also continued in Acts 28:30-31, long after premillennialism says it was postponed.

God's everlasting kingdom has continued, in different modes of administration, since it was introduced to us in the Garden of Eden and will continue on into "*a New Heaven and a New Earth*" forever. God will shake the universe once *Heb 12:26* and that shaking will destroy Canaan also.

As far as I can see the facts could not be clearer, the land promise was a type, of "*a New Heaven and a New Earth*", which also had to be fulfilled and was so in Joshua's day.

Joshua 21:43-45 "The Lord gave unto Israel <u>all the land</u> which he sware to give unto their fathers; and they possessed it and dwelt therein. V44 And the Lord gave them rest round about, according to all that he sware unto their fathers... V45 There failed not ought of any good thing which the Lord had spoken unto the house of Israel; <u>all came to pass</u>".

With the promised type fulfilled their remaining in the land was conditional on them meeting the threshold of obedience the covenant required. **Gen 17:1-2 *"I am the Almighty God; walk before Me, and be thou perfect. V2 And I will make My covenant with thee".***

They never could live up to it and broke it continually. However, God delayed finally taking the sceptre from them, until the coming of the Lord. The Lord was never going to be stuck in a failed contract. However, the believer is in the covenant that the Lord made with the Father, and which

He keeps perfectly. Neither Paul, Adam nor any man could keep a covenant of works Rom 7:17. Our Mediator, His sacrifice, priesthood and covenant are superior to the types in the Old Testament, *"The promises are yeah and amen in Christ"* 2Cor 1:20.

Before the sceptre was finally taken from them, they were sent temporarily into captivity to show that God cannot tolerate sin. These captivities were not permanent because the genealogy had to be fulfilled in Bethlehem, their captivity and return making this prophesy all the more remarkable. They were promised in each period of captivity that they would be restored back to the land which was fulfilled by their return from Babylon and Assyria and not in a future premillennial kingdom. The focus is on man's relationship with God, in Christ, not on man and his ethnicity.

It was providential that the filling up of Jewish apostasy would coincide with the fulfilment of the genealogy. Now no-one can ever again produce such evidence, biblical or otherwise, to support a claim to be the Messiah on earth. A premillennial messiah would lack this Biblical evidence also.

Premillennialism also overlooks the very reason that man was driven out of the Garden of Eden in the first place, which was to deny him access, in a fallen, sinful state, to *"the tree of life"*, Gen 3:22. A premillennial kingdom would allow flesh and blood access to the "*Tree of life*", something which just cannot be, 1Cor 15:50. The unbelieving Jew displays the same enmity to Christ and His people, as does the unbelieving Gentile, and will go to the same place if they die unrepentant.

The tree of life is said to be guarded by a "*flaming sword*" Gen 3:24, signifying that it will be inaccessible to natural man forever, Jew or otherwise. Canaan could be accessed by natural man.

The Lord will deliver but one kingdom up to His Father 1Cor 15:24: the everlasting kingdom. A premillennial kingdom of death and sin, however, is neither a victorious nor an everlasting kingdom.

Section Three

World history in miniature

Alongside the many visual aids, creation, and our conscience, God has woven historical narratives into His Word which provide us with a condensed view of world history, spanning from the Fall to "*a New Heaven and a New Earth*", showing exactly how all world history and the plan of salvation will pan out. It is a world history in which there is no room for a premillennial system, while at the same time proving rather that there has only ever been one way of salvation, one doctrine and one Gospel. It is impossible now for any other faith to have the same level of undeniable proof the Gospel has, which God has woven into history, creation, languages and His Word which can never be undone.

1   The Patriarchs

The Spiritual kingdom of God in the Old Testament is not separate from His spiritual kingdom in the New, *Mat 12:25*. If the Old Testament Jews, or those who are in a premillennial kingdom, so called, have not the Spirit of Christ, then they are none of His Rom 8:9.

The same 'good news' baton has been passed down throughout history, to the New Testament Church *1Cor 1:13*, explaining the same message as the visual aids, only more clearly now, we are not to go back to the more obscure. Hebrews 11 lists Old Testament men who all lived by faith, in the promised Messiah. We can take them as examples of what we should believe.

From the time of Adam onward God dealt directly with the Patriarchs, who were neither Jews nor Israelites, for around 2000 years, unveiling His plan to them and they in turn to the world. Noah (who was not a Jew) was a preacher of righteousness *2Pet 2:5*. It was the same Gospel that they then preached to Abraham and the Nation's fathers, *Gal 3:8 "Preached the Gospel unto Abraham"*, (who also was not a Jew). The Old Testament is not all about the Jews.

In the first phase of world history, we are given the greater picture in Adam the representative head of all mankind Acts 17:26, and his probationary period in Eden, which is then condensed for us in the life of Jacob, the representative head of the Nation, *Gen 13:15*. Jacob was living in the land promised to Abraham, but did not yet have ownership of it. Picturing Adam who broke his probation at the 'Fall', Jacob in *Gen 42:3* listened to the world's offer to meet his need, and went down into Egypt, only to end up being deceived and abused by the world, all of which was ordained by God, Gen 46:3-4, to bring His purposes to pass. Just as a sacrifice was made for Adam, so the Passover in *Ex 12:11* was made for the Nation. Pharaoh was punished for his crimes against God's people just as the Serpent was cursed for his.

God chose The Nation of Israel to showcase His dealings with mankind, in a real live drama presented to a now growing world audience. God has left nothing to chance or debate.

Firstly, coming out of Egypt onto the wilderness stage, and then dwelling in Canaan, a drama and narrative full of visual aids, props, names and place-names, all of which had spiritual meaning. Many in the Jewish Nation representing mankind, unwittingly played their own parts also.

Most of the Nation, thinking they had been chosen for their greatness, failed to see their individual need and embrace the message of salvation, or share it with the world, as they were supposed to. In fact, they had been chosen because they were "the fewest of all people" Deuteronomy 7:7, meaning the focus of attention would be on God's glory not their own. *"God takes the weak things"*.

In pride they learnt their own lines, while missing the overall storyline. In fact, along with the Remnant many in the Gentile audience, came to grasp the entire unfolding narrative of miracles, deliverances, blessings, and the Sabbath rest etc, *Num 14:14*, and believed God's word for themselves, eg: Naaman and the city of Nineveh etc. One way for all. Also, many in *Deut 23:1-3* who could not become part of the Nation, would still be able to enter into the spiritual kingdom of God.

Justification, *1Pet 3:18*, was pictured for us in their crossing of the Red Sea *Ex 14:21-26*. While sanctification is pictured in their wanderings through the wilderness as *"pilgrims and strangers"*, preparing a people for a prepared place in the Promised Land, picturing the glory *of "a New Heaven and a New Earth"*, which leaves no room for a premillennial kingdom in the Biblical narrative.

Num 21:8 Midway through their journey the Serpent is lifted up on a pole, picturing Calvary, the central event of world history where *"He became sin for us"*, and a look by faith secured healing.

Joshua 1:1, Moses representing the law, *Gal 3:24*, could bring them to the Promised Land but could not bring them in. It was Joshua, meaning saviour, who must bring them in. Those who were not worthy died in their sins and were shut outside, forever. It was not unconditional for them. Moses a saved man was also not allowed to enter the land, which shows it was an ideal picture only.

The Nations' entry, providentially, coincided with *"the filling up of the iniquity of the Amorites"*, the seed of Ham, *Gen 9:25*, picturing the final day of judgement, of reward or punishment, for all.

Gen 15:14-16 Just as the Amorites received judgement when their iniquity was filled up, so Israel's special protection was removed in 70AD when, killing the Lord, they apostatized and became as every other Nation *Matt 23:38*, which they were warned of in Deut 8:20. And so this world will receive judgement also when its iniquity is filled up.

While the core storyline remained the same, the curtain came down on scene one, Mat 23:38, and has now come up again in scene two, Mat 21:43.

The same message that the Remnant proclaimed from the beginning is now proclaimed to the world by the Church, *"And I, If I be lifted up, shall draw all men unto me" John 12:32.* The Gospel mantle of the Old Testament Prophets has now been passed down to the believers in the Church, 2Kings 2:13.

"The hour cometh and now is, when the true worshippers shall worship the Father in spirit and truth: for the Father seeketh such to worship Him. God is spirit and they that worship Him must worship Him in spirit and in truth." John 4:23-24.

This does not mean a change of religion, as many believe, but quite simply, that the era of the National visual aids is over and believers have now moved on to the period of clearer Gospel light, *1Cor 13:11.* The world does not need this national lesson repeated again, once was enough to show this picture lesson, with the Gospel now teaching the same message more clearly. God has always sought such spiritual worship

The Nation itself was a visual aid, an ideal picture only, which never could be perfect, *"There is none that doeth good" Rom 3:12.* Many seek after land but there is *"none that seek after God" Rom 3:10.*

God's dealings with Israel also ran for around 2000 years, the last 400 Old Testament years being silent, which should also tell us that the Jews are neither the focal point of scripture, nor the focal point of the world's 6000 years of history.

One of the reasons I believe that God preserves the Jews today, is to prevent the enemy airbrushing out these biblical truths which are woven into their past history, and also to prove God's power to keep them. We love them now as we would any people, but we don't give them false worldly hope.

There is no requirement for, nor benefit to, anyone today, to know whether they are of Jewish lineage or not, nor even where Canaan is located, never mind having to enter there for salvation.

Bear in mind that it was a mixed multitude making up the Nation of Israel, which had left Egypt, Ex 12:38, which also shows that the nation was an ideal picture and not the Spiritual children of God.

The history of the Nation of Israel, full of visual aids, was played out in real time and recorded for us, *Rom 15:4,* so that we like them might understand the message of salvation for our souls, *Rom 1:20, "The invisible... from the creation of the world... being understood by things that are made".* So, from the very beginning visual aids have been God's way of supporting the Gospel message in His Word.

Again, we can only conclude from this narrative that there is no place for a premillennial kingdom in God's plan. Rather the plan fits perfectly with the spiritual view of the kingdom at present. There was one Fall, one Cross, one judgement and there is one restoration to "a *New Heaven and a New Earth".*

2.   Steven's confession of faith

ICor 14:36 "Came the word of God out from you? Or came it to you only"?

There is a second narrative provided for us here in *Acts 7* where Steven deflates the pride of the Sanhedrin, the Jewish ruling party, by showing them their true record and humble origins, and God's longsuffering toward them, which is a different picture to the one they, or premillennialists paint.

They boasted of Abraham *Matt 3:9,* the promise, the land and the Temple. However, Steven takes them down through their Nation's history, showing how they inherited the Oracles from Gentile fathers Acts 7:38 and that the origin of their genealogy was neither Israeli nor Jewish.

He reminds them:-

*   V9 hat their nation also started badly, when their forefathers sold Joseph into Egypt, *Gen 50:20* "Ye thought evil against me, but God meant it for good". Like Abraham they have nothing of which to boast before God. In fact, their privileges make them more guilty.

- V33 That Moses met with God, on what at that time was Gentile "*holy ground*".
- V39 How they continually "*turned back in their hearts into Egypt*".
- V44 How, for forty years, the Tabernacle was confined to travelling through the wilderness.
- V45 Then, after entering Canaan till the end of David's reign, the tabernacle was moved around the land from tribe to tribe, showing it to be a temporary and transient arrangement only. And David still considered himself to be "*a sojourner*", even when dwelling in Canaan *Ps 39:12.*

  It was not until Solomon's reign that the pilgrim structure came to rest. Yet he declared that this is still not the reality, neither could it nor would it ever be!
- V48 "*How be it, the Most High dwelleth not in temples made with hands. V49 Heaven is my throne, and the earth my footstool*", the earth, and Canaan, is not His kingdom, but His footstool. Yet premillennialism would make a localised deity of the eternal One, with a stone building on a piece of local 'Real Estate', *2Chronicles 2:6,* which is what His enemies thought of Him. God's purposes are infinitely greater than a premillennial kingdom.

Then Steven draws the attention of the Sanhedrin to their murder of the Lord and his prophets.

- V52 "*When they heard these things, they were cut to the heart, and they gnashed on him with their teeth*". This is probably when they sealed their own spiritual death warrants and that of their Apostate Nation which they had signed at Calvary, *John 7:48 "Have any of the rulers believed?"*

Many interpret 1Cor 2:8 as saying that the unconverted princes would not have killed the Lord had they known who He was. When in fact, what is being said, is, had they known Him as their own personal Saviour, they would not have killed Him. They did not kill Him in error, as they knew what they were doing, John 11:50. It was Christs' spiritual reign that they, and many today, do not want.

Steven's murder by the Nation's ruling party and their final act of apostasy is suggested by many as the event that brings us to the end of Daniel's 70th week, Daniel 9:24: the Lord's death being the middle of the week, "causing [the need for] the sacrifices to cease" V27.

Daniel's 1st week was the promised return to and restoration in the land of Canaan which has been fulfilled, not a premillennial kingdom, years, later.

3.   The parable of the Tares

Mat 13:24 "The kingdom of Heaven is likened unto a man which sowed good seed in his field. V25 But while men slept his enemy came and sowed tares among his wheat. V28b wilt thou that we go then and gather them up? V29 Nay: lest while ye gather up the tares, ye root up the wheat also with them". V38 "The field is the world: the good seed are the children of the kingdom; but the tares are the children of the wicked one. V39 The enemy that sowed them is the devil; the harvest is the end of the world; and the reapers are the angels".

A third narrative is provided for us in the parable of the Tares, which speaks of Satan sowing his tares when deceiving Eve. But God did not and will not initiate the final judgement before the final harvest, and this parable tells us why, to avoid destroying the Wheat. There is one harvest day.

All three examples show that there is no room in history for a premillennial type kingdom or judgement. Rather they show that the antichristian system runs alongside the Gospel, in the New Testament age, revealing the constant enmity that we are to expect, there will be no separation of Wheat and Tares, while this world stands. *Joshua 24:15 "Choose ye this day, whom ye shall serve".*

The Wheat representing the godly seed of the woman can be traced in the Patriarchs and Prophets, Israel's Remnant, the genealogy, and now the

Church, all of whom are one people of God belonging *to "the everlasting kingdom"*. Notice the kingdom of <u>Heaven</u> includes us today V38.

The Tares representing the seed of the Serpent can be traced in Cain, Ham, Babel, the Pharisees, who are "of your father the devil", Judas the "son of perdition", the New Testament Judaizers, and the many antichrist Jew or Gentile who are unsaved and at enmity with believers, destined for "the Lake of fire". There are never three groups of people in the world but two, saved and unsaved.

I am told that Tares look like Wheat in the early stages, the only difference being that the Tare is empty on the inside, just like the Pharisees of *Mt 23:27* and any unsaved whether Jew or Gentile. When the Tare becomes distinguishable it is too late to separate them, as its roots are entangled with the Wheats'. *Lk 11:39 "Man looks on the outward appearance, while God looks on the heart"*.

God knows what He is doing, ordaining all things to bring about His own will Rom 8:28.

This world is the perfect environment for Him to produce the type of spiritual children that He wants, who, *"knowing good and evil"*, will choose Heavenly treasure over earthly 'Real estate', no matter what it costs, *"Consider my servant Job" Job 1:8*.

Our experiences on earth, and the fallout from sin, remind us of the Fall and Calvary and the price it took to redeem us. This causes us to lose faith in this world and look outside ourselves and this World to God for help Col 3:1. When we do, He saves and keeps us in this hostile *'wilderness'*, just as He kept the Nation of Israel, proving to onlookers, that they can trust Him for salvation also, while leaving those who reject Him without excuse. The Gospel is the primary focus of attention from now on not the visual aids. *"My sheep hear my voice, and I know them, and they follow me" John 10:27*.

This world is the worst the believer will ever know, but the best the unbeliever will ever know. My prayer is that it is NOT the best You will ever know!

A premillennial kingdom falls short of God's glory.

The believer sorrows for sin because it offends God *2Cor 7:10,* the world sorrows because of the consequences suffering and loss that they reap from sin, which will be forever if they do not repent.

Caesar was able to march into Canaan and conquer it with carnal weapons, while citizenship of the country can also be obtained by natural birth. However, the kingdom of God could only be purchased by Christ, and man can only obtain and enter it by spiritual new birth. While Moses was barred from entering Canaan, life was going on as normal for the citizens and traders, who were able to enter and exit the land with neither Angel nor flaming sword, barring their way, showing that the land itself was an ideal picture only, a working visual aid. There is no mention either of angels rejoicing over anyone entering Canaan. It never could be Eden restored.

The Gospel is the only message which reverses Eden, conquering our enemies and converting them to Christ, to serve Him, and bring glory to God. A premillennial kingdom fails completely to achieve this, and is of a completely different spirit. They will kill their enemies we pray for their conversion.

Section Four

Antichrist: the man of sin

Rev 17:17 "For God hath put it in their hearts to do His will, and to agree, and give their kingdom unto the beast, until the words of God shall be fulfilled".

Notice that there is not anything that happens which is not ordained of God to bring about His will.

Premillennialism teaches that *"Antichrist"* will come at a date in the future, when the Church has been removed. However, if we agree with this then we are unlikely to be aware of his presence and tactics in this present period. Their kingdom will be the *"Beasts"* until the fulfilment of God's Words.

There is much speculation as to whether *"Antichrist"* is a person or a system. Whether it refers to a period in the future, as premillennialism teaches, or to the here and now as I hope to show.

Also remember that just because you may not know who he is, does not mean that no one knows.

It calls for discernment and understanding. It is the number of a man, *666, Rev 13:18.* Indicating that his religion is man centred, based on the earthly and visible, which is just what premillennialism proposes for man. *"Antichrist"* is an anti-type of Christ but he is also a type of Satan, so he himself is not our final and ultimate enemy. Also, the number six can never be seven, the number of Divinity.

Many Christians are looking at the Middle East, famines, plagues and earthquakes as signs, but these are primarily signs for the world who will not read the Bible. We look primarily to the word of God which foretells the spiritual events we see unfolding, such as the spiritual decline in the world and the visible church. All the while God is still doing His marvellous work.

1John 2:18-22 "It is the last time... Antichrist shall come... even now... many antichrists, whereby... know it is the last time. 4:3 the spirit of antichrist... already is it in the world".

Certainly, an antichristian system has existed since our Lords Day, but 1John 2:18 would seem to clearly set "Antichrist" apart as an individual, of whom Satan himself has taken possession, who will head up this system possessed of lower ranking demons. As "*Antichrist*" does not have the definite article before it, it quite likely does refer to a succession of "*Antichrist*" as one dies another is raised up, each one in turn possessed of Satan, as he can only possess one person at a time.

Satan must have a man ready at all times as he doesn't know when the end will be, which would rule out it being just one individual at the close of history as opposed to a succession of individuals.

Notice also in V18, above, that the last period of world history began in our Lords Day and includes the period when "*Antichrist*" will come, the New Testament age, and not a pretribulation period at least 2000 years later.

"*Antichrist*" is identified for us as the Beast to whom the religious Beast gives its' power Rev 13:12-13 who sits as God. His revealing, I believe, occurred around 330 AD, with the union of the Beast of Constantine's Pagan Roman Empire and the Beast of the visible church, revealing antichrist the man of sin, who is against all that is called God, 2Th 2:3-8, which then developed into the Papal system.

Antichrist was no doubt in existence among the "*many antichrist*" before 330 AD, helping to bring the church to this point, but like Judas the "son of perdition", he had not yet been revealed publicly to all. The fact that the church joined with the secular power, is by default the church giving its power to the state Beast, *Rev 17:3.*

Up until 330 AD, Gods' Word was their authority, *which* the Holy Spirit used to restrain deception, giving the Gospel a chance to take root in the world Mat 24:14. The Lord would not return before this. With this falling away, the restraint was removed and they would "*believe a lie*" 2Thes 2:11.

The pope is the only one who unites the world and the religious globally in a wrong view of Christ. I can see no other contender for the title Antichrist who achieves all this.

The Pope himself claims to be the *'Vicar of Christ'.* Vicar actually means 'in the place of Christ. Another title of the Popes' is *'king of the Vatican'* and having a religious and political Concordat with the majority of countries in the world would certainly qualify him for the religious political role.

To claim to be in the place of Christ and claim His attributes is to usurp Christ, and "sit as God". Incidentally, this in no way infers that individual Roman Catholics desire to follow "Antichrist". I know this is not the case, as I grew up in the Roman Catholic church. Many are God fearing people, who I hope will come to a saving knowledge of the truth and find peace to their souls in Christ.

This goes also for premillennialism and many religious systems. In many cases, the student is master to the teacher, *"the people heard Him gladly"*, most leaders sadly did not.

However, until you find peace in Christ, you will inevitably choose what you think is the best of the rest, or simply stay with what you grew up in. *"Peace, peace when there is no peace"* Jer 6:14.

This falling away in 330 AD, will end with outright apostasy 2Pet 2:20-22, and the loosening of Satan to deceive the Nations spiritually, gathering them to Armageddon and judgement, *Rev 20:8.*

Mat 24:5 *"Many will come in my name saying, I am Christ. V26 here he is in the secret chamber".*

Premillennialism will say here he is on his throne *"sitting as God"*. The Roman Catholics say here he is in the Eucharist, or represented in their 'infallible' Vicar of Christ. The Muslims also say it is their messiah who returns to reign. We are to heed none of them, *Gal 1:6-12*, it is all one, it is Antichrist. Premillennialism is not able to tell us how anyone is to know whether it is Christ, or Antichrist imitating Christ, reigning in a sinful world. Death also means Satan is still active.

Just as Judas was aided by the religious leaders of his day, so we expect the false religious world leaders of today to be aiding Antichrist, " *Ye are of your father the devil"*.

In the same subtle manner that the Roman Catholic system attacks and substitutes every single Christian doctrine *2Th 2:3-4*, for example the sufficiency of the Cross, Spiritual worship, the Gospel, faith alone and repentance, so Antichrist seeks to remove them and replace them with Judaism, Roman Catholicism, premillennialism and every religion of works *2Th 8:15 "He is skilled in intrigue"*.

Antichrist's interest in Canaan 'Real estate' and "earthly treasure" is as tools to use in his primary goal of capturing men's souls. All the while premillennialism encourages man to focus on and squabble over this earthly terrain, *"Keep yourself unspotted from the world" James 1:27*.

Sadly, we are told in *Jer 5:31* that *"the teachers taught falsehood, and the people loved it so"*, and in *Isaiah 30:10,* they asked that he "*prophesy deceit*". Well, God will oblige them and will *"send them strong delusion, that they believe a lie" 2Th 2:11*. Today, they will "*not endure sound doctrine" either, 2Tim 4:1-4*. There is only one doctrine and Gospel that is sound, and it is not premillennialism.

2Tim 3:13 "But evil men and seducers shall wax worse and worse, deceiving and being deceived". The unsaved are able to identify the obviously wicked but it takes Biblical discernment to identify the evil seducer. John 7:17 *"If any man will do His will, he shall know of the doctrine*". It was not hard for the

Serpent to deceive Eve, or any disobedient person. The saved only truly learn through obedience.

It is not the most important thing to be able to identify who Antichrist is. If it were, it would be more clearly shown to us in scripture. The important thing is to be able to identify his false teaching and tactics. If we preach and defend the Gospel against all enemy, 'foreign and domestic', we will not miss hitting Antichrist also. This includes defending against premillennialism replacing our Gospel. It is Antichrist who would have us fight for Real estate and earthly treasure with carnal weapons, so as to render us ineffective, just as David would have been had he fought with Saul's sword etc.

It was once said, 'that the world will have any Jesus, whether it be a babe in the manger or in Mary's arms, the bread of the Eucharist, the prophet of the Mormons or Jehovah Witnesses, the warrior king of Islam and the premillennial kingdom, but not *"Jesus Christ and Him crucified"*.

Our Lord is the stone pictured in *Daniel 9*, Who conquers and reigns over the kingdoms of this world at His first Advent, and the One who the Jews rejected, *Mat 21:42*.

Rom 13:1 "The powers that be, are ordained of God".

How then are we to cope with the antichristian kingdoms and governments of the world? Especially as we witness this falling away. Unless we realise that Antichrist is operating now, we are more likely to be one of those deceived by his methods.

Remember though that God is sovereign, and "*all things work together, for good for them who love the Lord*", *Rom 8:28*. Not those who love 'Real estate'.

Daniel, Joseph and Moses worked for the governments of their day, setting an example for us, how we as believers are to deal with worldly governments and rulers, even trying to win them to Christ also. Many Christians continue to serve God faithfully in countries strongly opposed to the Gospel, which takes much wisdom and prayer. *Matt 22:21 "Render unto Caesar, the things which are Caesar's".*

2Tim 3:1-13 "In the last days perilous times shall come... V5 having a form of godliness, but denying the power thereof. V13 deceiving and being deceived"

We are to pray for the government of the day and pay taxes, whether it is an antichristian government or not, and it usually is Eph 6:12. We are to obey it where we can, except when its laws are against God's word. This has been the position since Nero's day. Corrie Ten Boom under Hitler is a more modern example of how to live in such regimes, hostile to the Gospel way of life.

Some Christians were deceived by Hitler's promise of an earthly, 1000-year Reich 'millennial reign'. So, we need to be sure we are able to identify and discern this spirit of antichrist, if we are to escape being entangled in compromise also. *"It is a form of godliness"*, which sometimes comes in the form of 'churchianity' with a smile, at other times in downright enmity, but certainly in deception.

The 1st Beast of Rev 13:1, is identified for us as the Harlot in Reve *17:1-18*, which is false religion, allied to secular power, *"with whom the kings of the earth have committed fornication".* In V3 we see her *"sit upon the beast"*, false religion and the world being now inseparable.

There seems little difference between the Beasts as they operate an uneasy alliance, heading up the world's antichristian systems while working toward the same goal, *"He that is not with me, is against me" Matt 12:30.* This is the state using religion and vice versa, to shore each other up.

Amongst other things Antichrist shall change the law given to the Jews *Daniel 7:23-25*; just as the religious leaders did, whom the Lord called *"ye generation of vipers"* in *Matt 23:33*, and who were "of their *"father the Devil"* *John 8:44*. They stopped others from going into the kingdom of heaven *Mat 23:13* all the while promoting Judaism which was this false view of the kingdom which was the precursor to Roman Catholic and premillennial teaching. It was not a material kingdom, but the spiritual kingdom that the leaders stopped them from going into. The true spiritual fathers focus was in the message conveyed by the visual aids. But Antichrist changes the focus to the visual, just as the Serpent did in the Garden of Eden. This inevitably results in deception and works based, worldly methods of worship infiltrating the visible church.

If another shall come in his own name, him ye will receive John 5:43.

We also hand power over to the Beast, and the spirit of antichrist when we look to the Government to legislate on spiritual matters or to deal with false religions and the moral state of the country; rather, our job is to preach the Gospel to them first. When we neglect to preach the Gospel, we leave a vacuum which is then filled by false religions.

When we plead with the government to give us equality in freedom of religion, expression, speech and democracy, we are inadvertently fighting for the equal rights of the enemies of the Gospel to preach their lies. (It seems it is Christianity which benefits least from this so-called equality anyhow!) Of course, we are not against true equality and freedom, but it is not always equally applied to us.

We do not seek the equality of the Gospel with other messages, as we know it is of infinitely greater value and power.

If we step outside the authority of the Gospel in the local Church, we introduce worldly methods for tackling spiritual problems, and the gates of hell have prevailed against us already.

Many are turning to protests in regard to moral issues, often alongside other religions, having lost faith in evangelism and Gospel preaching. We are not necessarily against protesting per se, but prevention is better than cure. The Gospel is the best way to deal with these issues. Protesting is more likely to force people to change outwardly only, rather than convert their souls.

Even when laws are made against the Gospel, we must continue to preach it rather than get side tracked into arguing about being allowed to preach it.

The Church does not make the laws of the land but by continuing to preach the Gospel, we influence those who have been given the sword, reminding and persuading them of their duty.

We are to focus on preaching the Gospel and not get side-tracked by anything, *"seek first the kingdom of God",* and God will take care of the rest. Do not lose faith in the Gospel.

These are the two versions of Christianity offered in the world today. The biblical one of separation from the world, and Antichrist's compromised churches of inclusive 'churchianity', adopting the worlds' culture and methods, opening the door to earthly thinking such as the premillennialist Orange Order members, his choirs, drum kits, concerts and telly-evangelists. Big names who pave the way for the one who has *"come in his own name"* (God didn't send him). Who create a clergy and laity mentality, and undermine the model of the local 'working church', at the coal face where diamonds are mined. Refer to 'the normative and regulative principles of worship' for guidance on this subject.

We must separate from and stand against worldly methods, or we are partaking of their sins also, *Eph 5:11 "Have no fellowship with the unfruitful works of darkness, rather reprove them".*

We are to be both wise and innocent, *Matt 10:16,* one without the other will not do, we cannot be innocent if we are not wise about what is right and what is wrong.

It is as clear to true believers that we should not be worshipping with members of the Orange Order, as it is that we cannot worship with Roman Catholics, John 9:41.

But there is none as blind as those who do not want to see.

2Th 2:7 "the mystery of iniquity doth already work".

The last days call for spiritual discernment in identifying Satan's methods of seduction and deception, in making evil sound good, and good sound wrong *Isaiah 5:20.*

The pace of life demands that we make choices quickly, which leaves those who have little time for prayer, meditation and bible study, easy meat for the great deceiver.

"There is one Mediator between God and men, the Man Christ Jesus" 1Timothy 2:5

It is as members of a local autonomous Church, under the authority of God's Word, that our responsibility lies. We do not make any such pledge to denominations, Unions, or any but Christ.

Be careful who you follow, for they will change direction, long before you realise. There is to be no earthly authority between us and God, outside of His word*, Rom 1:16.* It is the "*spirit of antichrist*" that seeks to unite all under one 'premillennial' type church and state. This *"spirit of antichrist" 1John 4:3,* has infiltrated many churches today, even influencing the world's view of the last days. I believe according to what I see in scripture, that a premillennial type, ecumenical Papal system will probably be Antichrist's final disguised attack upon the Gospel, though there will always be, "many antichrist" worldwide.

Deception is at its greatest when we don't realise we are being deceived, or don't think it is affecting us, when we are in fact promoting or condoning it, or just staying silent.

Gal 2:29 Born after the flesh, persecute those born after the spirit

There has never been any instruction given to stop preaching the Gospel while this world stands *Rom 11:25-26a,* plus we are to expect this enmity when we say the Gospel is the only truth. When we preach the Gospel, we are telling men what their conscience affirms is true, both Jew and Gentile have the same *"law written on his heart" Rom 2:15*, which affirms that the Gospel is true.

Deception means that the world does not suspect Antichrist, just as the Apostles did not suspect Judas, it calls for Biblical understanding.

A succession of individuals ties in with the progressively worsening cycles of Revelation, rather than a future event. Remember "there is nothing new under the Sun", it gets worse but is not different. If we remember that people will ask *"where is the promise of His coming?"* then this would indicate that things will continue much as they are, only progressively downward, morally and spiritually.

When religion and state really began to merge together in 330 AD, the Pagan world entered the visible church wholesale. Since then, there has been a progressive leaking of church authority to the world and state. This trend will continue with one character at the head of an ecumenical religious, political system till the end, which sounds very like a premillennial and Papal type system.

This is the picture of the two beasts presented to us in Revelation and it affects us today. This antichristian system will draw all those who lust after the here and now and the visible: premillennialism, Judaism, Paganism, environmentalist, astrologist, New Age, Roman Catholicism, Islam, Mormon, Jehovah Witness, Buddhist, those of all religions and none, uniting them against the true Gospel and Church. On which side does the premillennial view fit? Not the Gospels', Mat 12:30. The Christian faith is about a relationship with Christ, *"in Christ", Gal 3:26.* Every tactic of Satan's also involves man hoping to merit his salvation in some measure, *Rev 2:4 "Thou hast left thy first love".*

Our primary task is to examine ourselves, to see if we are in the faith, *2Cor 13:5*, and then to teach it to others, *"what think ye of Christ"?* Mat 22:42. I am ever conscious of the beam in my own eye Mat 17:3, knowing that *"He must increase but I must decrease"* John 3:30. It is a relationship, in Him, that we all need, Acts 20:21 *"Repentance toward God and faith toward our Lord Jesus Christ"*.

"The gates of hell will not prevail against it" Matt 16:18

The premillennial view will only encourage the unsaved to hope in himself and his future here.

Many people have lost faith in the Gospel to transform lives and so turn to premillennial type methods, compromised Churches, and parachurch organisations such as the Orange Order, social programmes, a health wealth and self-esteem gospel, which seem to be able to gather the crowds, *"Who hold down the truth in unrighteousness" Rom 1:18.*

The carnal man cannot see anything more important than what happens in the here and now, so the premillennial view provides what they want. But *"the just shall live by faith"*, Rom 1:17, in Christ.

It may not become noticeable for years but, at some stage, such parachurch organisations and earthly minded systems begin to think like businesses, fund raising to stay financially viable, needing to show success to their supporters, getting the best man for the job, rather than the most spiritual.

Though they may be sincere, the fact that they are not subject to the authority of the autonomous local Church leaves them as lone rangers, and the gates of Hell have prevailed against them already, *Numbers 32:23.* The Church is the only organisation that is ordained and instituted by Christ for the offence and defence of the Gospel, and which can truly call itself Christian.

The Church can be called Christian because relying on His Gospel, we are seen as perfect in Christ, by God, and will not be prevailed against spiritually. Can any other confirm that they will not be prevailed against? The Church alone will be preserved, while premillennialism and all unbiblical methods will not. Be careful you are not condemning yourself by what you allow, *Rom*

14:22. I am sorry if this sounds harsh but just look at how many organisations have apostatized, yet bear the name Christian. They were prevailed against, how? Was Christ defeated? No. They did not proceed in the way ordained of God, in His word. Premillennialism encourages this type of thinking by introducing the idea that preaching the Gospel is not the only way to bring about God's plan. Premillennialism is also akin to the false idea that an entire parish or country can be Christian.

When they go down, the name of Christ goes down with them. If the gates of hell can prevail against it, then whose is it? *Rev 2:10 "Be thou faithful unto death, and I will give thee a crown of life"*, trust in God's ways. We have a responsibility to those coming after to ensure that the Gospel is passed on. Someone once said, 'Teach your children biblical principles or the world will teach them theirs'.

While we are 'restricted' to the Gospel for worship *John 4:23,* and in the battle for men's *souls IJohn 4:1,* premillennialism uses the same language as the Serpent did and turns the hearts of men to carnal weapons and methods in a battle for Real Estate, and a shortcut to godliness Gen 3:5. This premillennial message has all the hallmarks of the ecumenical movement which undermines the Gospel when teaching that there is more than one way, and will be prevailed against. The Cross is an offence, *Gal 5:11,* to natural man, who is unable to humble himself and trust entirely on God for salvation. Satan's false offer allows man to do something for himself, choosing a powerful worldly leader and system he can be proud of, *"we have no king but Caesar" John 19:15. 2Cor 4:4 "The god of this world has blinded"* the false religious leaders, of this world. Many of them are easily identifiable by their earthly HQs such as Mecca, Jerusalem, the Vatican and Tibet *ICor 15:47.* The one thing they all have in common is that they have a wrong, low, view of Christ Who is both God and Man, and a high view of man, *"shall be as gods".* They all find unity here.

The premillennial kingdom is an earthly idea and will also have an earthly leader, but it will not be Christ, it will be Antichrist. How do we know it cannot be Christ? We know because the Sun will still be shining along with their, so called, premillennial kingdom, *"The Lamb is the light thereof"* Rev *21:23.* This world will accept Antichrist as messiah, to deliver earthly gain. All this being so, we expect to see *"many antichrist"* in this New Testament age, united on the "broad way" of ecumenism, with Antichrist numbered among them, developing and promoting his earthly kingdom, using such earthly methods outlined above. It is Antichrist alone who makes his kingdom of the visual, aesthetic here and now and that is what premillennialism is promoting. The Lord's kingdom is not the actual visual aids, but the spiritual kingdom conveyed by them.

There being only two kingdoms, Christ's and Antichrists, it is the premillennial kingdom which best fits the visible, earthly character, and spirit of Antichrist, first offered by the Serpent in Eden, and which we are told to expect in the last days, *"a form of godliness"*, 'religiosity'. As time goes on, I believe it will be increasingly obvious that all false religions are working toward this same goal.

If premillennialism were true, then it would create an abominable situation where it would be heresy to preach our Gospel in the millennium. That is exactly what Antichrist is promoting today, leading to the persecution of believers, which the bible speaks of, *"The time cometh, that whosoever killeth you will think he doeth God service"* John 16:2. Premillennialism advocates the same. If you are a Christian, then be careful you are not cutting off the very branch you stand on when you support premillennial teaching, which replaces the one true Gospel. You cannot serve both.

Rev 13:16 "The mark of the beast"

What then is the mark of the beast? Again, there is much speculation. Premillennialism plumbs again for the material rather than the spiritual, teaching that it is a visible mark. Quite simply, someone is said to have the *"the mark of the beast"* on their forehead when they are seduced and deceived into thinking in worldly ways *1John 2:15.* We need a renewed mind Rom 12:2. The mark on the right hand is then demonstrated when this develops into acting, worshipping and doing business like the world, which premillennialism and every other false religion promote, quite unlike the right hand of fellowship of the believer in *Gal 2:9*. Of course this does not mean that Satan will not suggest visible marks, which are a double bluff, to confuse us and take our minds off spiritual matters.

Ordinarily there is a general trend of enmity against the Christian anyhow, which makes it difficult for the Christian to do business. But alongside this, Satan is developing a more organised campaign of enmity against the Christian, making even buying and selling difficult *Rev 13:17*. Be prepared that many will think it strange if you don't compromise for expediency or unity, *1Pet 4:4*. Satan will also use such tactics to make us feel isolated. But you are not alone: *1Kings 19:18*. I'd rather fellowship with five true believers, than a house full of compromised professors. But worry not if business is hard, God will take care of those who seek to put Him first *Matt 6:33*. To love this present world and not the Gospel, or fear man more than God, is to have *"the mark of the beast"*, which is the spirit of antichrist. If someone professes faith but the bent of their life is not consistent with Gospel separation and practice, then they are to be considered unsaved, until the case is proven otherwise *1Cor 5:11*, "bringing forth fruit meet for repentance, Matt 3:8. Then they are to be accepted.

The binding of Satan

Rev 20:1-2 "And I saw an angel... having... a great chain in his hand. V2 And he laid hold on the dragon, that old serpent, which is the devil, and Satan and bound him a 1000 years":

Premillennialism says that Satan, who has the power of death *Heb 2:14*, cannot at present be bound, because of the evil and death that is in the world. Yet in their own kingdom teaching, they have the same sin and death *Rom 5:14*, a kingdom which even ends in war.

Mk 3:27 "No man can enter into a strong man's house and spoil his goods except he first bind the strong man, then he can spoil his goods". The Lord had to bind *"the prince of this world"* at His first Advent, before spoiling his goods and saving souls. *"I have finished the work which Thou gavest me to do" John 17:4.*

It is to be noted that Satan is a spirit and cannot be bound with a 'literal' metal chain, *Rev 20:1, it is all symbolic.* He has always been curtailed, in one respect or another. For example, when he was cast out of Heaven *Ez 28:16,* when needing permission against *Job 2:6,* when limited against the Nation of Israel, then at the Lord's first Advent *Mk 3:27,* when crushed and cast out at Calvary *John 12:31,* when needing permission to *sift Peter Lk 22:31,* and now by the preaching of the Gospel, his deceiving of the Nations is restrained, then he is loosed in *Rev 20:3,* to gather his own to judgement.

2Pet 2:4 "God spared not the angels that sinned, but cast them down to hell, and delivered them into chains of darkness, to be reserved unto judgement".

This verse alone scuppers the premillennial view, for it tells us that all of the fallen angels, which includes Satan, are at present bound by chains until judgement day. So, being loosed can only mean from limitation, not inactivity, as we know that the demons were active in the Gospel era, and still are. This all goes to support the 1000 years when Satan is bound, as being in this present period.

Even if Satan alone were bound in a premillennial kingdom as they suggest, his many minions would still carry out his dire bidding, as they always have done and would do in a numerical 1000 years.

Satan, a fallen angel, is *"The prince of the power of the air"*, *Eph 2:2*, and *the prince of this world John 12:31.* However he is neither king nor sovereign but is restrained under the *"King of Kings"*, *is* the origin of all evil and can only act to type, so is bound to do evil only, which God allows and channels to bring His own purposes to pass. Even the very Fall of mankind serves God's purposes.

Satan has no original positive thought, but *"is subtle" Gen 3:1.* Being able to *"masquerade as an angel of light" 2Cor 11:3,* he mimics God's ways while tainting them with wickedness, which means that religious systems such as the premillennial view can look right to many.

It seems that Satan is deluded into thinking he can win, especially when he sees believers fail. Although Satan has been in heaven, has seen the flood and the incarnation, he does not understand our spiritual victory and the relationship we have in Christ 1Pet 1:12.

He is not omnipresent, omnipotent, nor omniscient, and if we resist him, he will flee *James 4:7.* He cannot control the weather, nor is he able to read our minds but by a process of observation and elimination he can work out what causes us to fall.

Seeing how successfully the visual aids confuse man, he has no need to change strategy. Like premillennialism, Satan thinks he will have won when he captures the visual aids and Real Estate.

We love God's visible creation but the carnal covet it, which is idolatry, as it is all they have.

It must also be remembered that along with Satan, we have two other equally formidable enemies, the *"world which lieth in wickedness"*, and our own flesh, whose hearts are fertile seedbeds for sin *Jer 17:9.* Premillennialism gives us no idea how flesh could succeed in their premillennial kingdom.

Rev 20:7 "And when the 1000 years are expired, Satan shall be loosed out of his prison".

The loosening of Satan's chains at the end of the millennium is, the trigger for Armageddon, which is made up of a short period of time when even the very elect would be deceived, if possible, Mat 24:22-24, which is the climax to the falling away, and a famine of the Word, "Shall I find faith on the earth"? Satan is loosed he is not released. The Lords' reign has not ended, Satan is loosed to bring the Lords final purposes to pass.

The battle is first and foremost between the Godhead represented in Christ, and Satan.

Because Satan can do nothing to breach the Lord, *"hath nothing on me"* John *14:30*, he does the only thing he can: he attacks God's people, creation and Word.

Armageddon

**Rev 16:16 "And he gathered them together into a place which is called...
Armageddon.**

What then are we to make of Armageddon? Is it a physical 'pre-tribulation'
war between Jews and Gentiles? Or is it an earthly description of the climax
to the spiritual war between Christ, His Church and our spiritual enemies at
the end of the world, between the saved and the unsaved?

Many things militate against it being a physical battle. If Armageddon were
a physical battle, then the unsaved Gentile children, the sick, and elderly
from around the world would not be able to make it to one location for the
fight, so would remain alive and avoid being destroyed all of which scuppers
the premillennial view. It is symbolical of the spiritual battle and final
judgement.

The battle of Armageddon is a global climax to the ongoing spiritual battle
between those *"born again of the Spirit of God"*, and those born of the flesh
only, it is not a physical battle against the Jews, in one location, but is the
final judgement of all who oppose God. This does not detract from the fact
that evidence of this enmity and spiritual battle can be seen, in different
ways.

*Rev 19:19 "And I saw the beast, and the kings of the earth, and their armies,
gathered together to make war against him that sat on the horse and against
his armies".* By identifying with the Beast against Christ, all the wicked really
do in *Rev 16:16 and 19:19,* is separate themselves for judgement.

Premillennialism also has a problem when they insist in taking these two
verses chronologically, as they then end up with two 'end times' *"in the last
days",* as has been pointed out earlier.

Incidentally where do these end time rebels come from, if the Lord has been
reigning physically, as premillennialism teaches?

We seek to convert our enemies for Heaven by the preaching of the Gospel and by prayer *Lk 6:28*. But if premillennialism is right, we would need to prepare for a time when we will physically fight and kill God's enemies, in order to obtain earthly 'real estate'. The Lord's reply to premillennialism, would be, *"Ye know not what spirit ye are off"*, *Lk 9:54-55*, it is a spirit in opposition to the Gospel.

The Rapture

1 Thessalonians 4:16-17 "For the lord Himself shall descend from heaven with a <u>shout</u>, with the voice of the archangel, and with the trump of God: and the dead in Christ shall rise first: V17 Then we, which are alive and remain shall be caught up together with them in the clouds, to meet the Lord in the air: and so, shall we ever be with the lord.

A secret rapture is an integral part of premillennialism. While we are all in agreement that the Church will rise to meet the Lord in the air, John says it will be on the last day *John 6:39*, and it will be anything but secret, *"shout... voice... trump"*.

It may surprise some to know that there is no mention of a secret rapture in the scriptures. Also, the premillennial view of the rapture is more akin to the monastic idea of escaping from temptation.

Far from wanting to take us out of the world, the Lord prays that we are kept in the world, *John 17:15*. As a testimony to His saving power He leaves us here to influence the world, rather than removing us for fear the world would overcome us, *"We are more than conquerors"*, *Rom 8:37*.

Surely premillennialism would concede that the Lord's prayer to keep us in this world is answered?

It is as imperative now to the plan of salvation that we remain in this cursed world as it was that the Lord ever came into it. We are in the world, but we are not of the world, *John 17:16*.

We are to stay here to obey and preach the Gospel, which has a double-edged sword, one side of which justifies and saves the penitent while the other side condemns the unrepentant.

As we suffer persecution and temptation here, we are to take our comfort from the promise of the Lord's return *1Th 4:18*. We will not flee this battle field, neither will we stay and fight on worldly terms, using premillennial carnal methods and weapons, *2Cor 4:10*.

Abraham would not have it said that he took any worldly help. We have the *"whole armour of God"* and the *"sword of the Spirit"*, *Eph 6:11* and V17, weapons which are infinitely superior to those of our spiritual enemies. We see the weapons they use against us and the Bible tells us they will fail, Isaiah 54:17. So we will not change to using premillennial weaponry and methods.

In the parable of the ten virgins, the bride went out to meet the groom and accompany him back to where she had come from, which was the custom in the East.

So too at the rapture, the Bride will be lifted from the earth and graves, leaving behind those who call on 'mother earth' to cover them with her rocks, even as these rocks are being melted by the *"brightness of His coming"*, *2Th 2:8*. Adam tried to cover himself with fig leaves. What am I hoping to cover myself with? *"When I see the blood, I shall pass over you"* *Exodus 12:13*.

After we go out to meet the Lord, one party must go back with the other, so why would it not be us going back with the Lord, as we are to judge the world with Him also, *1Cor 6:2* at this stage.

The Lord returns once to judge and restore all things Acts 1:11, marking the end of the millennium. It can only be once *"in the fullness of time... gather... all things in Christ, both in Heaven and on earth"* *Eph 1:10*. The premillennial system needs it to be at least twice more. Heb 12:27 clearly tells us that He will shake the heaven and the earth but once more but Heb 1:13 tells us that the Lord is seated in Heaven until His enemies are made His footstool, which means it happens now. The entire earth will become His footstool in the restoration Isaiah 66:1, Lk 20:43.

Spiritually our souls are secure in heaven, *Eph 2:6,* until the Lord comes, when we will be glorified in body also, for the consummation of the marriage, enabling us to live in a glorified place, with Him, if we are "*Christ's at His coming", ICor 15:23.* We are not glorified, and then brought back to sinful earth for 1000 years.

There is but one return and final judgement, described in the bible *John 5:27-29, "once to die and after this the judgement"* Heb 9:27. "*The heavens and the earth, which are now... reserved unto fire against the day of judgement and perdition of ungodly men", 2Pet 3:7.* It is clear that the earth is not going to be destroyed and then restored again for a premillennial kingdom, then destroyed again, to then be restored again for *"a New Heaven and a New Earth".* They are reserved for fire once, after which they are reconstituted for the eternal state.

The Church will still be here looking for His coming *2Pet 3:12,* which is also in judgement, for "the Wicked at His coming" 2Th 1:7-10. Every eye shall be there to see it Rev 1:7. It is, quite simply that the judgement of the wicked and final deliverance of His people 1Th 1:9-10, is one event, namely what has become known as the rapture. We are raptured and Armageddon climaxes in final judgement and harvest.

The Gospel trumpet is the only "certain sound" that will cause Jew and Gentile alike to prepare for this, ICor 14:8: not the "strong delusion" taught in premillennialism.

I will be held accountable, and their blood will be on my head, "*If I preach not the Gospel",* or if I preach premillennialism "*another gospel, which is not another".*

The Lord will destroy all that is *"wood hay and stubble",* Heb 1:12 "*As a vesture shalt thou fold them up".* Then He will restore all things. All things here will be totally destroyed once, 2Pet 3:10-12.

There can be no room for sin and death when all things are renewed, and *"a New Heaven and a New Earth"*, is the only time and place where there are *"no more tears"*, death, sin or sorrow.

Just as premillennialism tries to divide the kingdom of Heaven from the kingdom of God, so they try to divide His second Coming and His appearing. However, these terms are used interchangeably, for the same event. *"The end of all things is at hand"* IPet 4:7.

Premillennialists do the same thing when they try to separate the Lord's kingship from His Headship, and when they try to separate the sheep, the wheat, the bride, the Remnant and the Church from each other, when in fact they are all different names for the one *"seed of the woman"* in Christ, introduced to us in the Garden of Eden, simply viewed from different aspects.

Premillennialism describes going back to Judaism and the visual aids as the restoration of all things. But Paul describes their going back to the visual aids as going back to *"beggarly elements... bondage"*, Gal 4:9; and "*carnal ordinances... imposed on them, until the time of restoration*" Heb 9:10. The restoration takes place after these things that were imposed on them are gone. Therefore, they cannot be the restoration. Imposed also means they were a burden hence the privileges were to offset this burden. The Lord could not have restored all things in a premillennial kingdom, *while the last enemy death"* still reigns. *"Nothing that defileth shall enter in"*, to "a New Heaven and a New Earth", but defilement can enter into their premillennial kingdom. You decide which is right.

As remarked earlier the premillennial system also has the Lord reigning and the Sun shining, together. However, we know this cannot be, as the Sun will be gone when Christ reigns physically, *Rev 21:23 "no need of* the Sun... *the Lamb is the light thereof"*. We know the Sun will only be removed when *"a New Heaven and a New Earth"* appears and this world including Canaan is gone and the Sun with it.

However, in order for the premillennial kingdom to have the Lord and a numerical 1000-year reign, which is 360,000 literal biblical days and nights, they need the Sun and the Lord to be here together.

It is also said that we will see the Lord *"face to face"* in *a New Heaven and a New Earth 1Cor 13:12,* Why would scripture say this if we had seen the Lord, face to face already for seven years in Heaven after a secret rapture, and for a 1000 years in a premillennial kingdom?

Again, there are far too many inconsistencies in the premillennial system, thus disproving this teaching, which just cannot be ignored.

It is the unbeliever who is caught out at the rapture when the Lord returns as a thief, not us. The only sign of the end that the world will be given is the progressively worsening cycles and falling away, as portrayed in Revelation. The true Christian is always ready, having trusted in Christ.

The Great Tribulation Matt 24:21.

John 17:15 "I pray not that thou shouldest take them out of the world, but that thou shouldest   keep them from the evil".

Premillennial dispensationalism teaches that the reason why God raptures His people is because He would not let us go through great tribulation, that it is reserved only for the wicked who have rejected Christ. Though they do actually have 'pre-tribulation' saints going through it.

Therefore, they insist that the Church must be removed from the earth, which was similar to the opinion of Job's false friends, and also the Lord's disciples, who believed that if you suffered it was because you were a sinner, *John 9:2,* and therefore God was against you.

They have absolutely no proof in scripture to base this tribulation idea on. The Lord said we are to *"occupy till I come Lk 19:13.* We will be here facing tribulation until the Lord returns. It is reckoned, that of the 53 times tribulation is mentioned, it is endured by the righteous 47 times, which is the enmity that we have been forewarned of. *"I send you forth as sheep in the midst of wolves"*, Mt 10:16.

The parable of the Wheat and the Tares, shows that we will exist here, alongside each other, until the Lord comes again to judge at the great harvest. The believer and the unbeliever will not at any time have the separate existences before the day of judgement that premillennialism bases itself on. Can it really be shown that no child of God has ever gone through great tribulation?
We are told "that all that will live godly, will suffer persecution*", 2Tim 3:12*. And that quite often, it will come from professing Christians, Matt 10:34. There has always been tribulation and falling away, but in the last days it will climax, to great tribulation *Mat 24:21*, and apostasy from the Gospel. Premillennialism will shelve the Gospel.

Rather what we will never suffer is this eternal wrath *Heb 13:5*, but we will suffer tribulation and persecution, at the hands of unbelievers, precisely because we will not waver, and give up the Gospel Heb 10:26. In fact Paul went through horrendous tribulation, as did the men of *Hebrews 11*. Not to mention, *"the last enemy, death" Heb 12*, which we all have to face if the Lord be not come.

Tribulation, along with the death and decaying of the body, are types continually reminding us that "the soul that sinneth, it shall die", *Ezekiel 18:20*. Death is the separation of the soul from the body *Rom 6:23*, while sin causes the separation of our soul from God. Our bodies will die but our souls need not die. These things are a necessary visible message in themselves to remind us of that.

Acts 14:22 tells us we must *"through much tribulation enter into the kingdom"*. Tribulation and death are a doorway to the eternal state for the believer*, "Oh death where is thy sting"? 1Cor 15:55*.

This premillennial attitude to suffering is contrary to Paul's attitude in *Rom 8:18*, and also in *2Cor 12:7-10 where* Paul asked three times for the thorn to be removed, but in V9 when God told him *"My grace is sufficient for thee"*,

Paul's response in V10 is "*Therefore I take pleasure in infirmities*", and our response should be the same.

God was basically asking Paul "Do you want Me to wrap you up in cotton wool? Or fix all the problems of the world, just for you, or take you out of it? Or do you want Me to give you 'great' grace to overcome this "*great tribulation*" here?" "*Count it all joy when you suffer persecution*", *James 1:2.* We are able to count it all joy in persecution, because such enmity reminds us that we are the Lord's, and He is on our side, *Heb 12:6, 10.* What is my answer? Premillennialism's response is either fix the worlds' problems, or take me out of it. Premillennialism would have us bypass suffering, just as Peter would have had the Lord avoid Calvary. However, we know the Lord's response to Peter, "*get thee behind me Satan*", *Matt 16:23.*

Satan shoots himself in the foot when he persecutes mankind, for it is then that many run to Christ for deliverance, "*All things work together for good, to them that love God*" Rom 8:28.

No matter how bad it gets, the Lord is able to keep us, "*not suffer you to be tempted above that ye are able*" *1Cor 10:13.* He uses suffering to wean us from sin and the world, thereby making us more useful in His spiritual kingdom, *John 15:2 "Purge... that you bring forth much more fruit".* Tribulation also shows others where the enmity is coming from, who it is directed at, and why.

In fact, it is probably because of tribulation faced by believers that many false professors will not join the Church Acts 5:13, thereby saving us from the havoc they would cause.

Tribulation causes us to draw near to God in prayer and to feel our dependence on Him. It is only when we understand the nature and purpose of suffering that it will help us with the task in hand, *Psalm 126:6.* If God had not shortened the time in 70AD, mankind would have destroyed itself. And it will be a short period again in these last days, when Satan is loosed to deceive the Nations, Rev 20:8, leading them to destruction, or even the very elect would be deceived if it were possible.

It is not possible that we can ever be deceived as far as the way of salvation is concerned. However, many are deceived into believing *"every wind and doctrine"*, from these false compromised preachers, *"Not everyone who says Lord, Lord, shall enter the kingdom" Mat 7:21*. There has always been deception, but in the last days it is climaxing in National deception, with governments making laws that favour sin and are against the Gospel. There is no neutral position.

We are pilgrims here, on a journey through the *"valley of the shadow of death" Psalm 23*. We are called to *"mortify the deeds of the flesh"* and to be *"living sacrifices"*, to *"take up your cross and follow me"*. It is when things are at their worst that we prove God most. This is not the type of attitude that the premillennial view engenders. 2Tim 2:12 *If we suffer, we shall also reign with Him"*.

We hold a different doctrine from the believers who hold the premillennial view, so one or other believer is being deceived in this matter. *"I know whom I have believed" 2Tim 1:12.*

There will be no hiding place on judgement day, when everything shall be made plain, *"Vengeance on them that know not God, and obey not the Gospel" 2Th 1:8.* There is no such condition to believe or obey premillennialism. They will not have this Gospel in their kingdom, so will have vengeance. The believer's obedience to the Gospel is twofold, to separate from the world unto Christ, and to teach it to others, no more no less. The great commission was not to preach premillennialism.

Rev 21:9 I will show thee, the bride the Lamb's wife. V10 And he showed me the holy Jerusalem. V22 I saw no temple therein: for The Lord God Almighty, and the Lamb are the temple thereof". V23 And the city had no need of the Sun... for the glory of God... and the Lamb is the light thereof". V27 "Shall in no wise enter... anything that defileth... But they which are written in the Lamb's book of life".

Premillennialism teaches that man is going to build the Temple again, for a premillennial kingdom. Again, they are confusing the visual aids, with the promised reality, Rom 8:24.

The Temple filled with the shekinah glory, its fixtures and fittings, and the sacrifices were a visual picture showing that there is One God and only one way to meet with Him, spiritually.

This Spiritual view is firstly borne out in V9-10 where we see that the bride is the holy Jerusalem and in V22 there is no Temple therein, God and the Lamb are the Temple thereof. So, no sacrifices either.

Secondly, if a premillennial Temple were built on earth, Heb 8:4 tells us that the Lord would not be able to serve in it, because if He were on earth, He should not be a priest, never mind a high priest. V1 but, *"He is our High Priest in Heaven: V2 A minister of the true tabernacle, which the Lord pitched, not man"*. So, who is the premillennialism high priest on earth? Who is able to go behind the veil for them? The same veil that was rent? Mat 27:51. We are told in V5, they are *"the example and shadow of the heavenly things"*, in other words, they were the visual aids to teach the spiritual. The high priest was a type of Christ, our Great High Priest Who has entered into the true Holy of Holies already. It is the Papacy that says God needs a physical representative here.

There is to be no Temple in *"a New Heaven and a New Earth"*, Rev 21:22. And the only one who will be serving in their so called premillennial, stone Temple will be Antichrist, *"sitting as God"*.

The Temple in the Old Testament was therefore a visual aid, a type of Christ and His church, in dwelt by the Holy Spirit, *"Christ in us, the hope of glory"*, *Col 1:27*, and us in Christ, *2Cor 5:17*.

Contrary to premillennial teaching, each individual believer in the Old Testament was indwelt by the Holy Spirit also, *1Pet 1:11*. They were then given a filling of the Holy Spirit for special missions, John 20:22, Acts 1:8. Like Nicodemus, if they are to be in the kingdom they must also be *"born again, of the Spirit of God"*. This requirement will be the same until the end of time.

Several things are apparent in *Rev 21:9*.

1. The Lamb's bride and wife are the same.
2. The bride is holy Jerusalem, V10.
3. The Godhead is the Temple. I believe the Lamb is mentioned separately in order to include the Human nature of the One crucified for us.
4. When the Lord is present, in all His glory, there is no need of the Sun.

In *Rev 21:10* we are shown *"the holy Jerusalem, descending down out of heaven from God"*, we are not to expect a stone Temple built by man *in a premillennial kingdom*.

In V12, we are told that the twelve tribes of Israel have their names written on the gates, and in V14, that the twelve Apostles have their names written on the foundations. Meaning that the Old Testament saints and the New

Testament saints are, indeed, all one people, in one place forever, which destroys the premillennial, two people of God, position.

It meant certain death for any other than the high priest to proceed beyond the "*Veil*". The Veil is Christ's flesh which was rent at Calvary, thereby opening up the way into the *"holiest of all'* for all believers, *Heb 10:20*. It is precisely because it was rent that we can now have access, in Him. The high priest going beyond the Veil was a picture of Christ taking us into Heaven. There is no one since Old Testament times who would qualify to enter the "most holy" Ex 26:31-35, beyond the veil, if it were to be repaired and exist in a premillennial kingdom's stone temple.

Premillennialism says that the Jews will repair the Veil, in a rebuilt temple, and renew the animal sacrifices again. Along with the middle wall of partition, a repaired Veil would actually block access to the "most holy", which was opened for us at Calvary. *"Ye shut up the kingdom of God against men"* *Matt 23:13. Psalm 127:1 tells us that if it is not the Lord who builds, then they build in vain.*

All through scripture, we are being trained to see the invisible reality by looking at the visible. The teaching contained in the 'visual aids' becomes progressively clearer as history unfolds, beginning with creation then the tree in the Garden of Eden, then the shadows, types, sacrifices, the Temple and furniture and the Nation of Israel, until the fulfilment Mat 5:17, and clear revelation of Jesus Christ *Heb 1:1.* And then finally it will be to glory where we will see Him face to face. The Lord says in Rev 1:8, "*I am Alpha and Omega*", someone has added, 'and everything in between'.

The temple priest had to stand, because his work was never finished, but Christ has finished His redemptive work and is seated at the right hand of the Father, Eph 1:20. Premillennialism would imply that it is not done. It is the Holy Spirit who then applies it now.

Any Temple now can have no Ark, manna, Aaron's budding rod, Veil, wall, or fire for their sacrifices, Lev 6:12. Any new fire now, will be strange fire and will be rejected, Lev 10:1-3. The temple certainly cannot have the full glory of God in it, as *"the heaven of heavens cannot contain Him"* *2Chron 2:6.* The Lord is building His Church with living stones, of which the Temple of stones was a type, *Matt 16:18 "I will build My Church".* There is nothing man can do, *"it is done".*

It is as clear to us that the Temple is a visual aid, as it is to premillennialism that the Bread and Wine are a visual aid. It is the same principle that needs to be applied to all the visual aids in the Bible. May God open our eyes to see this.

It was the *"chief corner stone" Eph 2:20,* that the Jews rejected, and still do, not the stone Temple which they love and idolise. Like all false religions, they love and covet the visual aid, not the Lord.

Circumcision

Rom 2:228-29 "For he is not a Jew, who is one outwardly; neither is that circumcision, which is outward in the flesh: V29 But he is a Jew, which is one inwardly; and circumcision is that of the heart, in the spirit, and not in the letter".

Fleshly circumcision is another integral part of premillennial teaching, where they fail to see the spiritual lesson being taught, V29. This circumcision never saved anyone, and never will, Deut 10:16. Broadly speaking, the Jewish Nation was Abraham's natural seed, circumcised in the flesh. But within the Nation of Israel there was the Remnant, the true Israel, the spiritual seed of Abraham, circumcised in heart, *Gal 3:29 "If ye be Christ's, then are ye Abraham's seed... heirs according to the promise".* A man could make his child a Jew, by circumcising the flesh, but it is God alone who makes any His child, by circumcision of heart, through the spiritual new birth only, Rom 2:25-29. The Nation of Israel was therefore an ideal picture only of Gods' dealings with all mankind, as many were proselytes Gen 17:23, and many were wicked. The Spiritual seed inherit the Spiritual promise.

Paul, wanting to give God all the glory, says, in effect, that if there is any reason why he was chosen, it is because he was the chief of sinners and nothing to do with his ethnicity at all, 1Tim 1:15.

Though he was still part of the Nation of Israel, *"My kinsmen according to the flesh" Rom 9:3*, he was also a part of the Church, which shows that there is not the division that premillennialism tries to create, between the Old Testament saints and the New Testament saints. Between the Remnant Jew and the unsaved Jew, yes. Not all Old Testament Jews were saints of God, by any means.

Paul warns us in *Phil 3:2* to beware of those teaching circumcision. He tells us he was circumcised on the 8th day V5, a circumcision which he now counts *"as dung" V7*.

He classes any who continue to promote this circumcision as "*enemies of the Cross" in V18*. Premillennialism teaching is promoting a return to circumcision of the flesh, and Paul would therefore class it as an enemy of the Cross. Who are we to argue?

Circumcision of the flesh gains entry into the Nation of Israel, but it does not gain entry into the kingdom of God and His holy presence. It merely cuts away the skin of procreation Col 2:6, while leaving man in his sin. It is *"circumcision of the heart"* V11 that cleanses us of all sin, which occurs when we are given a new heart, *Ez 36:26.*

Circumcision of the flesh is a type, teaching the need for circumcision of the heart, just as baptism today is a type teaching that we need our hearts washed inwardly. *Gal 6:15 Circumcision availeth nothing".* It does nothing to change the heart.

One is as clear to us as the other, that circumcision and baptism are both visual aids, and that there is no spiritual relief in these or any other visual aid, Heb 10:4.

Premillennialism, like Jewish circumcision, does away with the effects of the Cross, *Gal 5:11,* It is one or the other. It is the carnal who look on the visible types and shadows and forms his religion, from what he sees, and not from the message taught in them. Do not encourage them. *Gal 6:12 "As many as desire to make a fair show in the flesh... constrain you to be circumcised, only lest they... suffer persecution for the Cross of Christ".* This is what is behind every attempt to replace the Gospel. God has designed it this one way, so that it is easier to identify where each person stands. The unbeliever will not want to serve Christ if it is going to cost him. What about me, do I love Christ first, or do I love something else?

This antichristian characteristic can be seen in the worldly churches today, one of easy-believism, ashamed of the Gospel, with no stomach for separation, holy living, evangelism, defence of the Gospel Phil 1:17, and the authority of God's word. *"Having loved this present world"*, 2Tim 4:6. *"If ye live after the flesh, ye shall die" Rom 8:13,* premillennialism is after the flesh, and will cause any who trust in it for salvation to be lost 2Cor 3:7, and to die. Flesh and blood cannot inherit the kingdom of God", 1Cor 15:50. Premillennialism says that it is the kingdom of <u>God</u> that flesh inherits.

Rom 3:1-4 "What advantage then hath the Jew? or what profit circumcision? V2 Much every way: chiefly because unto them were committed the oracles of God".

Paul asks, then what was the purpose of such an elaborate National Jewish system, if these things did not save? V2 *"Much every way"*. Firstly, they were privileged with the Oracles of God and His direct dealings with them. Secondly, they had the great privilege of being the Nation that would see the Genealogy terminate within their Nation with the Coming of the Lord. Thirdly, that the privilege and purpose of the Nation was to be a visible testimony to the world, teaching them God's word and the way of salvation. They were blessed with great privileges to compensate for, and aid them in, this great responsibility, as we are today.

When they stopped, to idolize and make a religion of the visible, as premillennialism would have us to do, they became heretical, self-righteous and hypocritical, even turning it into *"damnable heresy"* 2Pet 2:1. Not all Old Testament saints in the spiritual kingdom, were in or belonged to the Nation.

The Old Testament saint and the New Testament saint.

Heb 8:6 "The mediator of a better covenant... established upon better promises".

Premillennialism argues that there had to be a different way of salvation in the Old Testament because they could not have known what we know in the New Testament, regarding Calvary.

If we look at the Genesis record, we can see that man knew more of the plan of salvation, from the beginning, than he is given credit for. That is, if we don't start with what the spiritually blind and dead did not know, but rather start with what the most godly did know, even that does not do justice to all that God has revealed in the Old Testament. *"There is nothing new under the Sun" Ecclesiastes 1:9.* Our covenant is better because the Lord now keeps it unconditionally for believers.

From the beginning, Adam was taught the fundamentals of the faith such as the Trinity, creation, Satan, sin, death, enmity, the tree of life and the need for a substitutionary atonement, which was pictured for us in *Gen 3:21 "The Lord God made coats of skin and clothed them".*

Adam and Eve were "grafted in again" after they fell, by trusting in the work of the promised "Seed" who was demonstrated in type, by the animal sacrifice. Every child of Adam since is born in sin and shapen in iniquity *Psalm 51:5,* in need of a Spiritual new birth. The Jews are no exception.

Of course, the Old Testament believers did not see Calvary as clearly as we do today. However, they did not see something entirely different. They looked by lamplight at the same Object as we see today, in the full light of day, even we still *"See through a glass darkly" ICor 13:12.*

It will take the full light of glory, forever, to unfold the meaning and depth of the eternal sacrifice of Calvary as we continue to learn more of the Infinite and eternal Godhead through Christ.

The journey for every saint in the New Testament is in the same direction, to the same destination, by the same Way as it was in the Old Testament. The Old Testament may be said to have travelled

by lamplight, lighting up the next step that they were to take. Whereas now, with the full light of New Testament scripture, we see further down the road but our next step is still the same as theirs was, 'the way of the Cross leads home'.

The animal skins taught Adam that if he is to live, God would have to provide a substitute to die in his stead. It is the same irreducible minimum required in the beginning as will be to the end.

Adam also knew that it had to be a man, *"the seed of the woman"*, who would redeem him. Yet he also knew that man and angel were subject to the Fall so neither could be relied upon, it must be God that does it all. *God shall provide Himself (as) a Lamb, Gen 22:8*. This is when the Gospel was clearly preached unto Abraham *Gal 3:8*. What God requires the Lord alone fulfils.

Although the mode of revelation, differed and became clearer through the ages, the Gospel message has never changed. It was the job of the Prophets, Apostles and preachers to explain the Gospel which was illustrated in the different modes of administration.

Eph 2:12-13 "That at that time, ye were without Christ, aliens from the commonwealth of Israel, strangers from the covenants of promise. V13 But now in Christ Jesus ye who were sometimes afar off, are made nigh by the blood of Christ". V16 one body. V19 fellow-citizens".

The Jew's first birth was marked by circumcision and entitled him to earthly promises only, just as our first birth graciously avails us of the earth's provisions and common access to the truth. It is the spiritual new birth alone which entitles any to the heavenly promise of eternal life and that goes for any in the Old Testament as well.

All of Abraham's seed are born naturally, and were a type of all men born naturally in Adam. These can be said to be children of the Father as Creator, but they are not the born-again spiritual children of God *Rom 9:8*, in Christ, *IJohn 3:9*.

God will always expect the same perfect standard of righteousness, which man cannot attain to. Our righteousness amounts only to self-righteousness, *"filthy rags"*. Thankfully there is a provided righteousness in Christ, if we will trust Him, He is my righteousness 1Cor 1:30. Premillennial righteousness earned by legal obedience is nothing other than man's own self-righteousness.

The Law

Gal 4:24-26 "Which things are an <u>allegory</u>: for these are the two covenants: the one from the Mount Sinai, which gendereth to bondage, which is Agar. V25 For this Agar is Mount Sinai in Arabia, and answereth to <u>Jerusalem which now</u> is, and is in <u>bondage</u> with her children". V26 But, <u>Jerusalem which is above</u> is free, which is the mother of us all".

Premillennialism teaches that we are not under the law today but that Judaism is the Jewish covenant that will return again, when man will earn salvation by legal obedience to the law. They mistakenly believe this because they think that the Jews earned salvation this way in the Old Testament period. The Judaizers taught this corrupt version of revealed faith.

What we have in Galatians is a comparison between this natural religion taught by Judaizers, which leads to bondage V25, and the Spiritual, which is free V26. *"In Adam all die, even so in Christ shall all be made alive"* 1Cor 15:22. These are really the only two covenants there are to choose from and it is obvious that premillennialism aligns itself with the earthly Jerusalem of V25 which leads to bondage. *1Cor 9:25 "They... obtain a corruptible crown; ... we an incorruptible".* This won't change.

When the Bible says we are not under the law today, it is referring to ceremonial and civil law, and supports the view that only the mode of administration changed, not the message.

But premillennialism also throws out the Gospel and the moral law, "*lawlessness*". We are under the law of Christ Gal 6:2, which is the *"schoolmaster that brings us unto Christ"*, and keeps us there. Though trying to keep the law will not save, it is the highest moral code and we try to live up to it.

Rom 4:14 makes it clear that if the law be heirs, then the promise is of none effect, it cannot be both. We need to be aware of the difference between the Spirit of the law, and the letter of the law.

There are really only two main covenants and people in the scriptures, one in Adam, and the other in Christ, the Last Adam", both were represented in the Jewish Nation. The Lord fulfilled His covenant as Kinsman to all mankind, saving all those who trust Him as Redeemer, *John 3:16*. The many different covenants pointed to the One promised. The Nation's focus was to be on Messiah (*"till Shiloh come"*), at which point the sceptre was to depart *Gen 49:10*, signifying the end of the use of the Nation's visual aids, *ICor 10:1*. This makes sense when we think that most Gentiles would not understand the National visual aids anyhow. The covenant that counts has to mean the same to all. *ICor 10:3"All eat the same spiritual meat. V4 same spiritual drink: and that Rock was Christ".*

Jas 2:10 "Whosoever shall keep the whole law, and yet offend in one point, is guilty of all". This verse causes a problem for premillennialism also, for either there will be a super race of Jews, equal to the Lord, who can keep all the law perfectly, without offending in one point, in their premillennial kingdom, or God will break His Word and lower His standards. Neither of which is possible.

The *"law is good, and holy"*. It is the law that discovers our ailment and sends us to the great Physician. There is only one and the same law, written on the heart of the Jew as is written on the heart of the Gentile. So, no matter who we preach the Gospel to, their conscience tells them it is true. Premillennialism is not said to be written on anyone's heart, confirming it.

We can never do enough to reach the Lord's perfect, righteous standard though we must try. *"Our righteousness is as filthy rags"*, Rom 7:19-21 *"When I would do good, evil is present there with me".*   The law shows that the flesh will always be a weak link in any system in which man is required to contribute. But thankfully we have *"a better covenant"*, one which Christ has kept for us.

Gal 3:17 "The covenant that was confirmed before of God <u>in Christ,</u> the law which was 430 years after, cannot disannul, that it should make the promise of non-effect. V18 For if the inheritance be of the law, it is no more of promise".

The law annexed to the covenant given in the Garden of Eden, was ratified 430 years later. No one was ever saved by the keeping of the law of works: it is one or the other. If it is of the works of the law, it is no longer of grace and promise *Rom 11:6.* Premillennialism, like Roman Catholicism, tries to mix these both, works and grace, together. The promise was of salvation to the penitent, trusting in Christ.

Gal 2:18 "If I build again the things I destroyed, I am become a transgressor. Building the Temple, the National law structure and the visual aids again would make man a transgressor.

Gal 3:19 *" The law was added because of transgression till the seed should come to whom the promise was made".* The law clarified and defined what had already been outlined as sinful.

It would be like introducing a 30mph speed restriction for cars in town centres, because previously there had only ever been the horse and cart that could not travel at 30 mph. The core requirement to drive safely had not changed. Neither do we earn anything by keeping this law.

Section Six

What is the premillennial gospel of the kingdom?

Rom 10:3 "Being ignorant of God's righteousness, and going about to establish their own righteousness, have not submitted themselves unto the righteousness of God".

We acknowledge that premillennialism takes the scriptures alone as their authority. But it is difficult to pin down what premillennialism teaches the gospel of their kingdom to be. At one time, they say it is when "*they will look upon me whom they have pierced, and they shall <u>mourn</u> for him"* Zec 12:10. But this is said to have been fulfilled in *John 19:34-37 "soldier... pierced his side... V36 For these things were done that the scriptures might be <u>fulfilled</u>... V37 And again another scripture saith, they shall look on him whom they have pierced".* They mourned over their sin here.

But Revelation 1:7 is regarding a different event at the end of the world, when every eye will see the Lord's Coming, and those who pierced Him (the unsaved) shall "*<u>wail</u>",* not repent.

On another occasion premillennialism teaches that the conditions of the Old Testament must be restored, which they say was salvation by legal obedience and the faithful keeping of the ceremonial law, which Paul calls *"beggarly elements".* No man can keep anything perfectly, except the Lord, and God requires perfection. No one in their kingdom, or any works religion, could be sure that they had achieved acceptance, Lk 17:10 *"Done all... still an unprofitable servant".*

The idea that there must have been another way in the Old Testament, comes from the mistaken belief that those who have never heard of Christ in the world must be able to come by another way, *Heb 10:4* implying that they could not have known in the Old Testament, that which we know in the New Testament. The hypothetical lost tribe in the Amazon jungle, is the usual example given for the belief that there must be another way for those who have never heard of Christ.

How can we respond to this? Firstly, I would say that this notion springs from not having a proper appreciation of the necessity of the Cross. The Cross was not just to rubber stamp all men's religions.   Secondly, every, so called, group of lost people that we have come across has shown signs of knowing something of Old Testament Gospel worship and the need for sacrifice. Take for example the Totem Pole of North America. It quite resembles the Serpent raised up in the wilderness. Or the stone altars of the Druids across Europe, which resemble the Old Testament stone Altars. Being all descended from Adam it is quite possible that these are Old Testament practises that have continued in raw form. It is not impossible that stories were handed down from generation to generation, as this type of story-telling was common before the written Word. The Chinese language and history contain much that would confirm this. God has woven His truth into history and language also. Lastly, I would say, that when man keeps using the light he has been given, God keeps giving him more, *Mat 25:28*, even bringing him to the point where he will find the Lord, John 14:6.

Elsewhere, premillennialism teaches that to enter the kingdom, your *"righteousness must exceed that of the Pharisees" Matt 5:20.* However, *"all our righteousness are as filthy rags" Is 64:6. And Rev 22:11 adds "let he which is filthy, be filthy still".* Of course, what the Lord said was hyperbole, as our 'best' righteousness would still only amount to self-righteousness.

Paul, a Pharisee, was *"touching the righteousness of the law, blameless" Phil 3:6.* So, if this standard was correct, it would exclude Paul, as neither he, nor anyone else, could exceed his own blameless righteousness. The Lord's righteousness, is the only one which *"exceeds the righteousness of the Pharisees"*. Which thankfully, He gives to everyone who believes *2Cor 5:21.*

Again, premillennialism teaches that Jews enter the kingdom because the promise made to them was unconditionally forever. However, many Jews have already been lost, so this could not be so.

Quite simply, the premillennial kingdom falls short of God's perfect standard, fulfilled only in Christ, everything was very good before the Fall, but in Christ it is now raised to perfection. Neither man nor this world could ever be perfect, we must wait for *"a New Heaven and a New Earth"* before we will see that, at which point everything is perfect in Christ for ever, even better than "very good". The fact that their system still has Satan means they still have the last enemy death also, 1Cor 15:26.

The Gospel

Gal 1:8 "Though we, or an angel from Heaven preach any other gospel unto you than that which we have preached unto you, let him be accursed".

Premillennialism teaches that our Gospel will be replaced by "the gospel of the kingdom" Matt 24:14, which, they say, is a different gospel to be preached by 'pretribulation' Jews. This is in keeping with the belief that there was a different way of salvation in the Old Testament. However, the early Church was made up initially of the "born again" Remnant of Israel, minus the National mode of administration, *"And so all Israel shall be saved" Rom 11:26.* God's dealings with His spiritual people continued on the same Gospel terms, "common to all" Jude 3-4. It is our Gospel light, alone, that dispels Satan's *"powers of darkness" Eph 6:12,* while the Gospel truth dispels his lies and deceit. The message never changed, so doesn't need to be changed back.

The reason that God did not judge man instantly after the Fall, is that His one plan was to gather a people out of this world, for His everlasting kingdom, in Christ, via the Gospel.

Also, Satan would have claimed that he had thwarted God's plan, had God destroyed man at that time, and saved none. Satan is still trying to thwart this plan when offering the premillennial kingdom, in place of God's Spiritual kingdom, and Gospel. Adding another plan adds confusion.

Premillennialism, like Roman Catholicism, is an elaborate system which undermines and replaces every aspect of the Gospel, while masquerading as angels of light, 1Cor 11:13.

Premillennialism contends that the gospel of the kingdom is a different gospel from our Gospel. But we have never been given any instruction to change or stop preaching the Gospel, quite the contrary, as can be seen In Paul's harsh response, *"Let him be accursed"*. Our Gospel is the same "good news" given by God in Eden, and the same one taking us right up to the end of the world. If there had been, or is, another way, then God would have used it, and the Lord need not have died. However, if premillennialism concedes that there is only one Gospel, then this would put every believer in the one body, as is the case and would destroy their case also.

We are told in Jude 3-4, that the message of salvation is common to all, and that it was once delivered. So, the burden of proof rests with premillennialism to show that this mandate has changed. There never has been two messages of salvation delivered.

In *1Kings 13:15-18,* The young prophet listened to the old prophet, saying the message had changed. *V15 "Come... with me...V16 I may not... V17 It was said... thou shalt not turn again. V18 I am a prophet... as thou art... an angel spake... saying bring him back... but he lied".* The religious can lie.

Several modern premillennial writers now see the problem that a different gospel causes and not wanting to be cut off from mainstream Christianity, claim it is actually the same gospel, even though they go on to attach a different doctrine to it, *"Wolves in sheep's clothing" Matt 7:15.*

I myself, had a similar experience to this. Once, when debating both a Unitarian and a Roman Catholic, I ended by commenting that at least two of us must be wrong, as we believed three different gospels. They were both incensed with me, insisting that we all believed the same gospel, even though our doctrine of the Person and sufficiency of Christ, was 'infinitely' different.

As with premillennialism and all false teachers, they mistakenly believe that they can separate the one Gospel of Christ from the one doctrine of Christ, *"There shall be false teachers among you"* 2Pet 2:1. The carnal man will always be *"carried about with every wind and doctrine"* Eph 4:14.

Like produces like, and not a different species, we will always reap what we sow, *Gal 6:7*. When the Gospel seed is planted, it takes root, and will always grow to produce the same doctrine, which expands upon and explains what has happened to the believer and how we are to live, ultimately producing a people able to live in the presence of God, *2Cor 5:17*. Good doctrine causes good growth, which blossoms into fruit bearing seed and so the cycle continues. Heb 13:8 *"He is the same yesterday, today and forever".* Premillennial doctrine is different and has therefore come from the roots of another gospel, *"which is not another".* To teach premillennialism is to be disobedient, 1Tim 1:3 *"teach no other doctrine"*, no matter how old their tradition is. This is something that is reinforced over and over again.

"Repent ye therefore and be converted that your sins may be blotted out" *Acts 3:19*. There has only ever been one, distinct, persuasive message for the unbeliever, *"Believe in the Lord Jesus Christ and you shall be saved"* Acts 16:31, and there only ever will be. Neither is the Gospel to be separated from the moral law, which uncovers our sinful heart to us, convicts us of sin, and draws us to Christ, otherwise we would never realise how sinful we are: *"the heart is deceitful above all things, and desperately wicked, who can know it"*, Jer 17:9.

The Apostles, and the Bereans of *Acts 17:11*, only had the writings of the Old Testament Prophets. What they found was that Paul and the Gospel taught the same thing, *1Cor 15:1-7*, and that the Gospel fully explained what the visual aids were picturing, it was the promise of Christ. There are many "New" things in scripture, but never, a new gospel or doctrine.

It must be emphasised that the offer of another kingdom and gospel did not originate with Judaism, Darby or Roman Catholicism. It began right back in the Garden of Eden, when the Serpent persuaded Eve to look and lust after the visual, rather than trust in the spiritual lesson being conveyed. It is the same deception which has been re-packaged and renamed, down through the rolling centuries, in Paganism, Judaism, Roman Catholicism and every false religion, climaxing in a Papal type premillennial kingdom system, which is the antichristian system we have been told to expect in *"the last days"*:- a works based, religion, making idols of the visual aids while claiming to have Christ presiding over it. Satan has been twisting scripture from the beginning, and will continue to do so.

Ever since *Gen 4:6,* man's flesh has wanted this false gospel. In Isaiah's day they wanted him to "*Speak unto us smooth things, prophesy deceit*" Isaiah 30:10. In Jeremiah's day, the "Prophets, prophesy falsely... and my people love it so" Jer 5:31. In Paul's day they would *"not endure sound doctrine; but after their own lusts shall heap to themselves teachers having itching ears. V4 And they shall turn away their ears from the truth unto fables"* 2Tim 4:3: What about us today? do we love it so? Would I accept a change of Gospel?

The premillennial system, by its own admission, is neither Christian nor our Christian Gospel. It is *"another gospel which is not another"*. As darkness cannot exist alongside light, it is inevitable that premillennialism tries to remove the true Gospel light in order to pass their own gospel off as true. The cuckoo will always take over the entire nest eventually, pushing the true chicks out.

"For he hath made him to be sin for us, who knew no sin, that we might become the righteousness of God in him" 2Cor 5:21. By paying my debt for sin, He keeps me from being sent to Hell, by robing me in His righteousness, He fits me for Heaven, taking me off the broad way and placing me on the narrow way. In *Isaiah 53:11* when the Father was satisfied that the debt had been fully paid, the wrath ceased. Being aware that the wrath had ceased, the Lord cried, *"It is finished"* John 19:30. The Divine sacrifice consumed the fire,

it had burned out on Him. It is finished as far as God is concerned, and God cannot lie. Is it finished for you?

God is satisfied in Christ's sacrifice, there is no hope in the idolatrous "*broken cisterns*"? *Jer 2:13.* There is nothing more for Him to do, to secure salvation, and certainly no requirement on Him to see corruption again, in the humiliating circumstances of a sinful sub-standard premillennial kingdom, so-called. *"He was obedient unto death, even the death of the Cross" Phil 2:8.*

We have been entrusted with preaching the Gospel, to overcome and convert our enemy: "*I am not ashamed of the Gospel" Rom 1:16.* Invading Canaan does not achieve this. *"The weapons of our warfare, are not carnal… to the pulling down of strongholds", 2Cor 10:4.* Premillennial weapons are carnal. 'Force a man against his will, and he'll be of the same opinion still'.

We can do nothing to qualify for salvation, other than trust in Christ. If I will repent, He will save me. *"A new heart… and a new spirit will I put within you" Ez 36:26.* Premillennialism will not save any. Salvation and entry into the spiritual kingdom are one and the same thing, it is not entry into Canaan. Angels do not rejoice because someone enters Canaan. It is spiritual warfare.

Section Seven

"The great white throne"

There is but one Throne and one day of judgement, when all mankind will stand before God. There is but one throne with different names, *Rev 8:22 "The throne of God and the Lamb"*. Not multiple as premillennialism teaches, *Heb 12:26 "Yet once more I shake not the earth only but also heaven".* The books of judgement are opened once in Rev 20:12, not twice, or more as premillennialism suggests. There can only be one perfect restoration, of all things, which would do away with death and sin. Therefore a premillennial kingdom where sin and death have returned, cannot be a perfect restoration. *"A New Heavens and a New Earth wherein dwelleth righteousness",* is perfect.

We will all stand before the *"Judge of all the earth" Genesis 18:25*, to give an account of the deeds done in the flesh. Like every Christian I lived a sinful life before conversion, 1Cor 6:11, but I thank God that He brought me to see and trust in the Gospel being conveyed in the visual aids. And though we are weak, we now hate the sin that we once loved. It is my sincere longing that this booklet, may also be of help, to some dear soul, in bringing them to this end also.

If your hope is in the premillennial system, or any other system, then you need to repent of your sins and trust in the finished work of the Cross, yielding your life to Christ, and He will save you.

Come out of her my people.

Rev 18:2 "Babylon the great has fallen. V4 come out of her... that ye be not partakers of her sins"

The Lord is not talking here about coming out of one stone structure and going into another but about getting our hearts and churches out of the world, and the world out of our hearts and churches, "*Come out from among them, and touch not the unclean thing*", 2Corinthians 6:17.

There are also many other ways than premillennialism where Churches compromise the Gospel today and have "*sin in the camp*". We are to (lovingly) separate from them and any who will not separate from them until they change, "*Have no fellowship with the unfruitful works of darkness*". If we do not separate, we are partakers of their sins, Eph 5:7-21, and will get burnt Prov 6:27.

Although there will always be enmity between the believer and the enemy of God we will live together here, until God finally separates those of spiritual new birth from those of natural birth only, at the harvest of "*the great white throne*", Rev 20:11: the goats from the sheep, the small from the great, the Tares from the Wheat. "*Depart from me, I never knew you*" Matthew 7:21. Only those who are born again of the Spirit of God, who are in Christ, will enter into "*a New Heaven and a New Earth*" John 3:5. Any trusting in a premillennial system for salvation will be lost.

This world, as is, will only continue until the Lord has finished building His Church, with living stones.

I know the great fear I had when I realised that I belonged to a system preaching another gospel. If I had been deceived about what I was so sure of all my life, then how do I know who to believe?

The answer is in the question. To some extent, we each put too much faith in our own wisdom, or the wisdom of others, rather than trusting in the Word of God, *1Cor 1:25*, or we fear man, or loss overly much *Proverbs 29:25*, "*Fear not little flock*" 2Kings 12:32.

We can all look back at decisions made when we silenced our conscience in a 'little' matter, opening the door to greater deception. Do not ignore the warning signs. Obey in the little things which you are sure of and God will trust you with greater knowledge of the way of salvation. Thankfully having trusted in Christ, He will never leave us again, *Heb 13:5*. And not only that, but He disentangles us from this world's mess and will *"restore again the years that the locust has eaten", Joel 2:25*.

I believe the debates about literalism, Israel and the church and Darbyism, to be red herrings. The premillennial false gospel did not originate with themselves, nor with Darby or Schofield either, as previously pointed out, but with the Serpent in the Garden of Eden. Debating about them only takes our energy and focus away from the true Gospel, which is the only message our loved ones, and this perishing world, need. The Devil does not care what we are fighting about, as long as we keep on fighting. Paul said, *"I want to know nothing, save Jesus Christ and Him crucified" 1Cor 2:2*.

A premillennial type gospel is what the Serpent offered Eve in the Garden of Eden, which is a perfect match for the antichristian message of deceit that will corrupt and ensnare many in these last days, *Gal 6:8, "Are ye so foolish having begun in the Spirit are ye now made perfect by the flesh", Gal 3:3.* How can any believer truly think that natural man can be perfected by the flesh?

John 17:4 "I have glorified thee on earth". The Lord Who is both God and Man, cannot now be separated from His Cross work, nor does He need to reign in the premillennial kingdom 'to show how it should be done'. *'It is done"*, He has never left us, and never will, if we are His, *Heb 13:5.*

Overall, the scriptures favour the view that the New Testament period is the millennium, and that our Gospel will remain until the consummation of all things at the end of this economy, at which stage this fallen, groaning creation Rom 8:22, the visual aid given to all, will be destroyed, having served its purpose. Just as the visual aids given to the Jews were destroyed in 70AD at the end of the Old Testament economy having served theirs, *"We cannot serve God and mammon" Mat 6:24*. The premillennial system is mammon. "Choose ye this day whom ye shall serve" Joshua 24:15.

Conclusion

If the "*whole world lieth in wickedness*" at the end, does the Lord lose? Will there be more in Hell, than in Heaven? Someone once remarked that he had read the end of the book, and God wins.

The Devil's strategy always backfires. One example of this is the number of abortions carried out in the world each year, estimated to be anything up to 73 million children.

Based on the account of David, in *2Samuel 12:23*, we believe that these children go to be with the Lord in heaven. There are other possible scenarios we could also give, to support the idea that there will be more in Heaven than in Hell, more than we can count, *Rev 7:9*. However when it comes to those who have reached the age of discernment, sadly there are few that find salvation *Mat 7:14*.

My hope is that this booklet will clear away the mysticism surrounding this theme and that we would all see the spiritual nature of the warfare and kingdom we are in and preach the Gospel. We must be convinced by scriptural reasoning and not by the traditions of any men, whether it is premillennialism, Roman Catholicism or any other; even if they have popular orators, own great aesthetic structures, *ICor 13:1*., or have a large following.

Premillennialism is a works based system conforming peoples' minds to this world, Rom 12:2, which takes them away from trusting in the sole sufficiency of the Cross, and from seeing that our soul's salvation is a purely spiritual matter.

If there could have been any other way, then our Lord need not have been humiliated by taking on flesh, becoming a servant to sinful man, submitting to death, *"Even the death of the Cross" Phil 2:8,* and the grave. But we thank God that He did, and that He rose again and is seated at the right hand of the Father, interceding for all who trust in Him, Rom 8:34.

We are in the last days of seduction and deception, the soul is still our greatest concern, not 'Real Estate', 'the good is enemy to the best'. We must be able to discern between what is right and what is nearly right, what looks and sounds right, but is actually wrong and compromised, 1Sam 16:7 *"Man looketh on the outward appearance, but God looketh on the heart".* Like the tree in the Garden of Eden, the sacrifices and visual aids teach us of the knowledge of good and evil, Heb 10:4. They could not take away sin themselves but point us to Christ, and Him alone.

I could have written a booklet on each component part and multiplied the texts in favour of the Biblical view and against the premillennial view. But I hope that what I have written will suffice, and be of help to any who might be struggling with premillennialism, and compromise in their Church. I therefore conclude that the millennium is primarily spiritual and that it is the New Testament Gospel age, which is the only chance to seek the Lord. Judgement will come next and then the end, a New Heaven and a New Earth, forever. All other ways are on the Broad way that leads to destruction.

Use your time and energy seeking to find the Lord, and waste no more time on *"broken cisterns". "How shall we escape if we neglect so great salvation" Heb 2:3,* we will not, there will be no purgatory, premillennial or re-incarnation escape route. *"Now is the day of salvation" 2Cor 6:2.*

"Ask for the old paths, where is the good way, and walk therein, and ye shall find rest for your souls", Jer 6:16-19. May every reader find rest to their soul, in Christ alone.

Even so come Lord Jesus, **Rev 22:20**

Additional copies available from

www.pauldkinney.com

Contact the author

paul@pauldkinney.com